Evolution and Crime

Human physique and behaviour have been shaped by the pressures of natural selection. This is received wisdom in all scientifically informed circles. Currently, the topic of crime is rarely touched upon in textbooks on evolution and the topic of evolution rarely even mentioned in criminology textbooks. This book for the first time explores how an evolution-informed criminology has clear implications for enhancing our understanding of criminal law, crime and criminal behaviour.

This book is directed more towards students of criminology than students of evolution. It is suggested that there is scope for more collaborative work, with criminologists and crime scientists exposed to Darwinian thought having much to gain. What is suggested is simply that such thinking provides a fresh perspective. If that perspective yields only a fraction of the understanding when applied to crime that it has elsewhere in science, the effort will have been worthwhile.

The authors attempt to provide a modest appraisal of the potential contribution that a more welcoming approach to the evolutionary perspective would make to criminology; both theoretically (by expanding understanding of the complexity of the origins of behaviour labelled criminal) and practically (where the evolutionary approach can be utilised to inform crime control policy and practice). An evolutionary lens is applied to diverse criminological topics such as the origins of criminal law, female crime, violence, and environmental factors involved in crime causation.

Jason Roach is a Chartered Psychologist and Reader in Crime and Policing at the University of Huddersfield. He has worked for the UK Home Office, taught at the Crime Reduction College and worked in various mental health settings. He has published work on various criminological topics including criminal investigative practice, homicide and violent crime, terrorism and Offender Self-Selection.

Ken Pease is a Chartered Forensic Psychologist and currently Visiting Professor and Fellow of University College London and Visiting Professor at the University of Loughborough.

Crime Science Series
Edited by Richard Wortley
University College, London

Crime science is a new way of thinking about and responding to the problem of crime in society. The distinctive nature of crime science is captured in the name.

First, crime science is about crime. Instead of the usual focus in criminology on the characteristics of the criminal offender, crime science is concerned with the characteristics of the criminal event. The analysis shifts from the distant causes of criminality – biological makeup, upbringing, social disadvantage and the like – to the near causes of crime. Crime scientists are interested in why, where, when and how particular crimes occur. They examine trends and patterns in crime in order to devise immediate and practical strategies to disrupt these patterns.

Second, crime science is about science. Many traditional responses to crime control are unsystematic, reactive and populist, too often based on untested assumptions about what works. In contrast crime science advocates an evidence-based, problem-solving approach to crime control. Adopting the scientific method, crime scientists collect data on crime, generate hypotheses about observed crime trends, devise interventions to respond to crime problems, and test the adequacy of those interventions.

Crime science is utilitarian in its orientation and multidisciplinary in its foundations. Crime scientists actively engage with front-line criminal justice practitioners to reduce crime by making it more difficult for individuals to offend, and making it more likely that they will be detected if they do offend. To achieve these objectives, crime science draws on disciplines from both the social and physical sciences, including criminology, sociology, psychology, geography, economics, architecture, industrial design, epidemiology, computer science, mathematics, engineering and biology.

1. Superhighway Robbery
Graeme R. Newman and Ronald V. Clarke

2. Crime Reduction and Problem-oriented Policing
Edited by Karen Bullock and Nick Tilley

3. Crime Science
New Approaches to Preventing and Detecting Crime
Edited by Melissa J. Smith and Nick Tilley

Evolution and Crime

Jason Roach and Ken Pease

Routledge
Taylor & Francis Group

LONDON AND NEW YORK

First published 2013
by Routledge
2 Park Square, Milton Park, Abingdon, Oxon, OX14 4RN

Simultaneously published in the USA and Canada
by Routledge
711 Third Avenue, New York, NY 10017

Routledge is an imprint of the Taylor & Francis Group, an informa business

British Library Cataloguing in Publication Data
A catalogue record for this book is available from the British Library

Library of Congress Cataloging-in-Publication Data
Roach, Jason, 1969-
  Evolution and crime / Jason Roach and Ken Pease.
    pages cm
  1. Criminal anthropology. 2. Criminology. 3. Human evolution.
  4. Criminal behavior—Genetic aspects. 5. Evolution (Biology) and the social sciences. I. Pease, K. (Kenneth) II. Title.
  HV6035.R63 2013
  364.2'4—dc23

                                                        2012041258

ISBN: 978-1-84392-392-3 (hbk)
ISBN: 978-1-84392-391-6 (pbk)
ISBN: 978-0-203-10108-7 (ebk)

Typeset in Times New Roman
by RefineCatch Limited, Bungay, Suffolk

For Matthew, Maddie, Heidi and Jack

Contents

Illustrations

Preface

The physique and behaviour of all organisms, including humans, has been shaped by the pressures of natural selection. This is received wisdom in scientifically informed circles. Currently, the topic of crime is rarely touched upon in textbooks on evolution and the topic of evolution rarely mentioned in criminology textbooks. This book represents an attempt to present, in a form accessible to social science students with no background in the biological sciences, the ways in which a Darwinian perspective has rich potential in enhancing our understanding of the criminal law, crime and criminality.

The book begins with a brief outline of evolutionary thinking (i.e. natural and sexual selection) and common opposition to it, before moving to the question of why criminology has, so far, proven resistant to this mode of thought. These reasons include a perceived need to remain true to the tradition of human malleability by social context, the fear of racist eugenics and the equation of natural selection with biological determinism. Given its fruitfulness elsewhere in biological and social science (evolutionary psychology is arguably the fastest growing and most exciting perspective in social science), it is only a matter of time before conventional criminology comes to be informed by the evolutionary perspective, or floats further down the backwaters of academic life.

It would be stupid to suggest that evolutionary thinking provides a sufficient basis for the study of crime and criminality. That claim is not made here. Yet such thinking does provide a perspective now absent from almost all undergraduate programmes in criminology. If applying that perspective yields a fraction of the understanding when applied to crime that it has elsewhere in science, the effort will have been worthwhile.

This book is directed primarily towards students of criminology, professional or amateur, not students of evolution. The writers' hope is that it will lead the criminologists of tomorrow to be more receptive to collaborative work alongside those with an evolution-informed way of thinking. Their discipline would become more exciting in the process.

So what must we do to persuade criminologists to take a more sympathetic approach to the evolutionary perspective? We have taken a two-stage approach. In the first, we seek to engender a sense of wonder at the complexity of the foundations of crime-linked behaviour, from altruism to law-making to law-breaking.

The resulting image of people as ultra-social super-cooperators provides an essential backcloth to a proper appreciation of deviance from the pro-social. In the book's second stage, we apply Darwinian knowledge and theorising to some of the traditional topics in criminology, where an evolutionary lens is applied to diverse criminological topics such as gender and crime, violence and situational crime reduction.

Acknowledgements

Since we had the initial idea for this book one of us has had two more children and the other has welcomed three new grandchildren into the world. As it took us so long to write this book, we have had ample time to call in favours and test the patience of more people than we have space to mention. We therefore must reserve individual thanks for those most burdened by us, but offer the remainder a collective big thank you.

First, we would like to thank Nicola and Routledge for their patience with us, especially as they inherited us from Willan Publishing. Second, we offer a big thank you to our friends and peers, Paul Ekblom, Aiden Sidebottom and Richard Wortley, who have encouraged us to commit our thoughts and inclinations to paper and reassured us that it was all worth it.

There are reasons why the book took so long, despite being a simple intro-duction to the topic. The research moved too fast for us to keep up! This is not an experience for which traditional criminology prepared us. If you are inclined to look at the years in which the work we cite was published, you will find that most of it dates from the last decade or so. We challenge anyone to point to a criminology text with such recent published work. For all its undoubted faults, the book reflects a frantic, desperate attempt to be up to date, or more realistically as little out of date as is feasible in an extremely active research area.

Jason thanks his wife Clare and son Matthew for putting up with his constant preoccupation and *occasional* moods when writing this book over the past four years. Also his thanks go to Maddie and Heidi (his and Clare's new arrivals) who have got off lightly really by only arriving in 2012 and so have only had to endure the last five months of Daddy staring into space. He loves you all very much.

Ken would like to thank Barbara Nelson and Ann Wright for acting as intelligent non-specialist readers, to check on comprehensibility. He's grateful to Bilkis Begum for pointing him towards central aspects of Islamic moral teaching. Anne Campbell kindly made available a pre-publication copy of her work. These have been referenced in the text as Campbell (personal communication). Terrie Moffitt pointed him towards sources of recent epigenetic research. He would further like to thank his dogs Spud, Steffie and Polly for enriching his life while he helped Jason write the book. Polly's death after a long illness in January 2012 turned

Ken's contribution to the book into a form of much-needed distraction from the bereavement.

Finally, we feel obliged to make an anticipatory apology. Several times in writing this, we felt we had written something original, only to find with further reading that the credit for originality lay elsewhere. There are without doubt points in the text where we have hypothesised or speculated without the appropriate citation, simply because we remained ignorant of the prior work. To all those against whom we have sinned in this way, please let us know. We are willing to spend nights in the Amazon warehouse adding citations by hand.

Finally, finally (inserted after editing without Ken's knowledge) I would like to pay tribute to my friend, mentor and co-author, Professor Ken Pease OBE, a man whose genius is only overshadowed by his warmth and kindness. Ken, writing this book with you has been an honour and a pleasure, but please can I go home now? J.

1   Crime and evolution

Strange companions?

The process of natural selection is proposed to have shaped many behaviors that represent crimes in modern societies, such as murder, assault, rape, and theft, to address ancestrally recurrent conflicts between individuals. The cost-inflicting strategies that we recognize as crimes may have been favored by natural selection when they gave individuals an advantage in competition for scarce, reproductively relevant resources.

(Duntley and Shackelford, 2008, p. 373)

Introduction

Let us get the definitions over and done with first. Crimes are actions in breach of criminal law as it applies at a particular time and place, however strange, misguided or brutal the law in question seems to us now. Evolution is defined here as the process whereby attributes of plants or animals, including people, become changed over generations by selection pressures operating on random genetic mutations, such that those best equipped to survive and bring their offspring to reproductive maturity feature in increased numbers as time goes by. Some more detail about how this might happen is given in Chapter 2 but, if you feel you need a little more clarity, please go to http://darwintunes.org/. There you will find both a simple account of the theory of evolution and (in an experiment called 'Survival of the Funkiest') you can trace the process whereby random sound sequences are transformed (over three thousand generations at the time of writing) into something approximating music by repeated selection amongst the variants. The end result is by no means a Bach Mass or an REM song, but it's probably better than many things you have downloaded. Darwintunes is a neat practical demonstration of how evolution works. The topic of evolution is rarely touched upon in criminology textbooks. The topic of crime is rarely touched upon *as such* in textbooks on evolution, but much of the material in them has clear implications for our understanding of crime. Criminology would certainly be the more reluctant partner in any foreseeable liaison with evolutionary science. This book is therefore directed towards students of criminology and not towards students of evolution, both because we think criminology is missing a trick by its neglect of evolution, and because we are not equipped to contribute anything (except our admiration for its ingenuity) to evolutionary thinking. We believe that there is scope for more collaborative work, with criminologists and crime scientists exposed to Darwinian thought having much to gain. It would be stupid to suggest that evolutionary thinking provides a sufficient basis for the study of crime and criminality, and that claim is not made. But we do think that such thinking provides a fresh perspective, a potential paradigm shift. Not for nothing was the Natural Science Museum in London's exhibition in 2008–2009 called the 'Darwin Big Idea' exhibition. Evolutionary ideas have seeped into virtually all biological sciences. Searching the website of the magazine *New Scientist* on the word 'evolution' yielded 298 hits for the year previous to the date of writing this in June 2012. That amounts to an average of six hits per weekly issue. These dealt with topics as diverse as the implications of evolutionary thinking for medical practice through its consequences for errors in decision-making to its adoption as a method of product design.

Thinking outside the comfort zone

Some word combinations make obvious sense, for example delicious food, high mountain, close friend. Some word combinations make sense only if you think hard enough. Good poetry contains many examples of this, and the use of metaphor reveals unexpected connections between different ideas. Then there are some word combinations that don't seem to belong together at all, however hard one thinks: fishy bicycle, geological porridge, bovine paperclip. For many readers, the words evolution and crime just will not seem to belong together. The words sound as strange in combination as the bovine paperclip. This perception of strangeness is not limited to people coming to criminology for the first time, far from it. Many of those who have spent a lifetime studying crime will find the combination just as strange. There are many reasons for this. They include the following beliefs.

1   *The theory of evolution is wrong because it is at odds with religious teachings.* According to this view, evolution doesn't just *sound* wrong when paired with the word crime, it sounds wrong when paired with *anything*. The idea of evolution, given this way of thinking, just *is* wrong and cannot be countenanced at any price for any conceivable explanatory purpose. Passionate rejection of this kind usually stems from perceived incompatibility with religious precepts. The principal religious objections seem to be that Darwinian evolution requires a longer past for the Earth than most major religions allow, and that it denies humankind a special, privileged place among living things. There is also the more practical concern that if we are shown to be beasts like other beasts, our behaviour will inevitably be bestial.

2   *Culture is obviously the most important factor in shaping people.* Almost everyone is born with arms and legs. Within limits, body shape is indeed determined by genetics and the environment of the womb. Many of those who are prepared to accept that evolution gave us our size and shape draw the line at our behaviour. An evolutionary account of human nature is often taken

to imply that people are fixed into a uniform way of behaving, which contrasts with the diversity of human language, art, etiquette and dispositions that we see around us every day. Debates about this tend to get entwined with concerns about free will. If evolution has shaped the ways you think, act and feel, the argument goes, free will cannot exist. As we will see, the notion that evolutionary thought makes for uniform behaviour is just wrong. Our preferred analogy is between behaviour and wood. Wood has a grain. Anyone who has ever worked with wood will tell you how much easier it is to work with the grain than across the grain. Evolution provides the grain for behaviour, but we don't have to work with it. Parenthood is a long-term exercise in subtly working with or against the grain of the behaviour presented by one's children. Working against the grain takes longer, but if a parent's principles dictate that it should be so, it is done. This is part of the reason why we don't encounter many twenty-year-olds with temper tantrums. But there is a definite grain to behaviour. We evolved a preference for sweet foods which was sensible when food was scarce in the late Pleistocene era. This preference was late Pleistocene appropriate (LPA) but is disastrous if indulged now, and the resulting obesity epidemic is in consequence taking its toll on health, particularly in western countries. Sensible eating goes against the grain of evolved human preferences. The same interplay between lifestyle, ecology and genetics is evident for other food preferences, and reveals the 'nothing but culture' perspective as just silly. Take the further example of lactose intolerance. People with lactose intolerance become ill when they eat dairy products. Lactose intolerance was the rule rather than the exception until humans became farmers, keeping animals which gave milk. This introduced a selection advantage for people who were lactose tolerant, so that lactose tolerance increased in frequency until now it is lactose intolerance that is relatively uncommon (Krebs, 2009). This does not mean that people are obliged to drink milk! The grain of behaviour changed as the organisation of food supply changed.

3   *To link crime and evolution is to make a category error.* This seems to be, for many social scientists, the clinching argument. Those making this criticism may be willing to accept the notion that people have evolved structure and some basic reflexes and simple behaviours. The ability to hold things, throw things and speak a language may be a product of evolved attributes necessary to such skills, like an opposable thumb or a descended larynx. Crime, such critics assert, is different. It is not a specific attribute or kind of behaviour, it is a *label* that society puts on a range of very different behaviours, from fraud to murder to stealing cars to blowing-up buildings. Linking crime to evolution is, according to this point of view, to make what philosophers call a category error. Categories are logical types, and a distinct set of ideas and tools are appropriate for each. The category error is committed when one makes a statement about something in one category that can only be said of something in another category. For example, to talk of pious wallpaper is a category error because only sentient creatures can be pious (if your wallpaper talks to

you about its feelings, of course, this is not a category error). If you had a tour of a hospital and visited the wards, the accident and emergency department, the maternity wing and the pathology laboratory, and you then asked 'Where's the hospital?' you'd be making a category error. A hospital is a different kind of thing to its components. A person is a different kind of thing to a collection of organs and a different way of talking and thinking about the whole person is appropriate. Governments enact laws and fund a criminal justice system to punish those who break them. Crime is thus a social construct, built by people, and consisting of the actions that are defined as against the law, in all their diversity. This changes from time to time, like fashions in clothes and music. The commission of crime thus belongs in a different logical category to evolution-shaped characteristics like the urge to fight or flee when confronted with danger (assuming you are prepared for the moment to accept that as evolution-driven; you would probably not be a survivor of the evolutionary process if that were not the case). Persisting with a category error gets you nowhere, and so linking crime with evolutionary pressures will thus, it is claimed, get you nowhere. We will argue that talking about crime and evolution together is not to make a category error. We will contend that the existence and enforcement of criminal law represents a mechanism (with evolved roots) whereby levels of cooperative behaviour necessary to sustain complex societies are assured. Fish, it is joked, are the last to recognise the existence of water. Similarly we will assert what you can see for yourself but may have forgotten to be amazed by, namely that humans are by a distance the most sociable and cooperative of mammals. Look around you to see who is talking to, or tweeting, whom. Even in lectures, the urge to communicate with those sitting nearby often seems overwhelming, especially to the poor sap trying to give the lecture. In short, thinking about crime and evolution together is not a category error, because the designation of the scope of crime is, however brutally and imperfectly it is done at a particular place and time, that society's specification of what needs to be done to counter threats to the mutual trust and cooperation necessary for a group to function.

4   *Evolutionary thinking eventually leads to genocide.* The phrase 'survival of the fittest' was coined by Herbert Spencer, not by Darwin, though regrettably it is linked with the latter name. Spencer perverted evolutionary thinking into a strand of social theorising termed 'Social Darwinism' (Spencer, 1870). If it had been called Social Spencerism, perhaps a lot of suffering might have been avoided. Put crudely, Social Spencerism held that people flourished or died according to whether they were or were not among the 'fittest', and thus helping the needy was contrary to what Nature had ordained. Darwin's own view (Darwin, 1871) was that the intentional neglect of the weak and helpless was a 'certain and great present evil' (p. 169). The notion of fitness came to be spuriously applied to whole categories of people, Jews by apologists for an Aryan master race, Hutus by Tutsis, Bosnians by Serbs. Actual or attempted genocide has been the outcome. To stress the point, such abominations were based upon ideas in the Spencer and Francis Galton (Galton, 1869) tradition

rather than upon a reading of Darwin. The image of Adolf Hitler with a well-thumbed copy of *On the origin of species* is ludicrous. If the Holocaust had been based upon Social Darwinism, it would have involved an initial misreading of Darwin's position, and a further perversion of his thought. The misreading might conceivably lead to a laissez-faire position ('let the unfit die, it's what Nature intended') – although, as noted above, Darwin explicitly rejected such a view – but not to 'kill the allegedly unfit'. A fine history of the evolution idea has been written by Oldroyd (1983).

There are adequate rejoinders to each of the above arguments except the first, where no amount of evidence will tilt the scales towards belief in evolution. As for the second and third, one of the delights of evolutionary thinking is how readily it accommodates diversity, both within and between species. In fact diversity is the necessary condition of evolution. Without initial diversity, there is nothing for selection pressure to work on.

Notwithstanding the mountain of evidence, the objections to evolution are held with much passion, and began in Darwin's lifetime. A famous debate in Oxford in 1860 pitched Thomas Huxley (pro-evolution) against the Bishop of Oxford, Samuel Wilberforce. During the debate Wilberforce asked Huxley whether he was descended from an ape on his mother's side or his father's side. Huxley countered that he would rather be descended from an ape than a man who misused his great talents to suppress debate (Jensen, 1991). The strength of the antipathy held on religious grounds has remained immense. In 1925, John T. Scopes was arrested for teaching evolution at Rhea County High School in Dayton, Tennessee. When the famous 'monkey trial' ended, Scopes was convicted of violating a law that made it a crime to teach any theory that denies the story of the Divine Creation of man as taught in the Bible and holds instead that man is descended from a lower order of animals (Leinisch, 2007). The complete transcript of the trial makes fascinating reading and remains available on the Web.[1]

Just a week before writing this, one of us was giving a talk at a college in the north of England, and asked two of the lecturers in psychology who worked there whether they taught anything about evolution. One answered 'No, and we'd be in trouble if we did'. As Michael Berkman and his colleagues observed, 'community pressures place significant stress on teachers as they try to teach evolution, stresses that can lead them to de-emphasise, downplay or ignore the topic' (Berkman *et al.*, 2008 p. 922). Perhaps the saddest aspect of this is the assumption of a right not to be offended. There is no such right. Behaving as though there were is disastrous for freedom of speech and thought.

One of us mentioned to a distinguished professor of criminology that our next project was to write a book on evolution and crime, and the reply was a look of derision and a scathing 'You're better than that'. That was probably intended as a compliment, but accurately reflects what most criminologists would think about the combination of ideas. Insofar as those studying and teaching criminology hold these views, they will not regard it as important or appropriate or even defensible to learn about evolutionary theory. It may not even be going too far to say that doing so might endanger their careers. Googling 'attacks on evolution' will give you a sense of the irrational content and vitriolic tone of opponents.

It is no surprise that Anthony Walsh and Lee Ellis, when surveying participants at the American Society of Criminology's 1998 meeting, found those attending demonstrated a troubling ignorance of biological science (Ellis and Walsh, 1999). A similar attempt by one of the writers of this book to ask questions about what criminologists knew and thought about evolution (at the British Society of Criminology meeting of 2008) received a frankly hostile reception. How are we to understand such a response? Apart from the specific reason mentioned above (it's a category error) we speculate that criminology's traditional roots represent the main obstacle to openness to evolutionary thinking. There are green shoots. For example, Richard Wortley's recent book (Wortley, 2011) deals at length with the topic. Bruce Schneier's even more recent book (Schneier, 2012) is suffused with evolutionary thinking. But the mainstream position of the discipline remains much as it was in 2003, when Walsh and Ellis wrote:

> In criminology, environmentalism is the assumption that variations in criminal behaviour result only from environmental factors, especially social environmental factors. The biosocial perspective is quite different. It assumes that biological and environmental factors interact to affect criminal behaviour. . . . Among the strongest supporters of the environmentalist view are criminologists with considerable training in sociology.
>
> (Walsh and Ellis, 2003, p. 1)

While passionate rejection is common amongst professional criminologists, what about the views of criminology students and others early in careers studying crime? They haven't had long enough in the business to develop strong prejudices. The central reason for such people failing to link evolution and crime, we speculate, is simply that they have not had the ideas placed alongside each other. If they are fortunate enough to have been exposed to both topics in their previous education, the subjects will usually have been taught by different teachers in different parts of the school and college curriculum, using different concepts and vocabularies, and so will never be fused in the student's thought process, however receptive she might be to such fusion. The ideas belong, as the jargon goes, in different frames of reference. This less malign interpretation of reasons for misunderstanding seems to be shared by Jerry Coyne (Coyne, 2009) who writes of a

> simple lack of awareness of the weight and variety of evidence in [the theory's] favour. . . . most of my university students, who supposedly learned evolution in high school, come to my courses knowing almost nothing of this central organising theory of biology
>
> (p. xix)

If that is true of biology students, how much more true will it be of students of criminology? It will probably take a generation for the antipathy towards taking an evolutionary view of crime to subside, and it will only do so then if new criminologists are informed of relevant aspects of evolution theorising.

While we will be writing specifically about evolution and crime, it is perhaps worth pausing to argue the case from a different perspective: that considering very different ideas alongside each other is valuable, and not just in the context of crime and evolution. Linking diverse mindsets is the essence of creative thinking.

Idea fusion and creativity

Our first task is to show that putting together ideas from different frames of reference often provides the key to understanding them. That it represents the essence of creativity. Our second task is to show that evolution is a frame of reference which has consistently been fruitful in advancing scientific understanding, so it is worth the effort to apply this particular set of ideas to the understanding of crime.

In his famous book *The act of creation* (1964) Arthur Koestler described many different examples of invention and discovery, and concluded that they all shared a characteristic which he called 'bisociation', which involved blending elements from different frames of reference. A good example is given by the Wright brothers' success as pioneers of powered flight. When they were not trying to fly, the brothers ran a bicycle repair shop. Cycle riders have to lean into corners. Aircraft, likewise, must tilt while turning, a fact which the Wrights' competitors had not fully grasped. Only by making the analogy with the bicycle could the Wright brothers design a viable, steerable aircraft (Johnson-Laird, 2005, pp. 32–33). Kevin Dunbar (K. Dunbar, 1995) and his colleagues (Green *et al.,* 2010) showed that thinking with analogies is widespread, perhaps universal, amongst scientists, and went some way to showing the brain functioning which underpins the process. The less obvious the analogy, they showed, the more fruitful it *may* turn out to be.

Creative people following the Wright route have usually had to weather criticism from those who think more narrowly. For example, the inventor of the jet engine, Sir Frank Whittle, failed to gain support for its development. As his obituary in the *Daily Telegraph* on 10 August 1996 notes:

> Although [the 1941 first test flight of a jet powered aircraft] was a moment of triumph for Whittle, it was tinged with some bitterness, for he had had to overcome years of obstruction from the authorities, lack of funding for and faith in his brilliant ideas. He felt, with justification, that if he had been taken seriously earlier, Britain would have been able to develop jets before the Second World War broke out.

Countless similar stories can be told, for inventions as diverse as the battle tank to the clockwork radio. So taking ideas from one frame of reference and applying them to another is in principle a good idea, but will not win the innovator any popularity contests. Of course, though, it depends on the quality of the frames of reference. Linking crime with alchemy or necromancy will not help understanding, except of fraudsters who claim skills in those enterprises. So we must champion the heuristic value of evolutionary thinking. Does it yield testable ideas? Is evolution a true account of how we got to be as we are?

Is evolution true?

Yes, it is. If it were not, there would be no point in making creative connections with it.

US Senator Daniel Patrick Moynihan is credited with the wise words 'You are entitled to your own opinion. But you are not entitled to your own facts'.[2] In a measured review of the evidence, the US National Academy of Sciences came down unequivocally on the side of evolution as true, for animals including humans.

> Opinion polls show that many people believe that divine intervention actively guided the evolution of human beings. Science cannot comment on the role that supernatural forces might play in human affairs. But scientific investigations have concluded that the same forces responsible for the evolution of all other life forms on Earth can account for the evolution of human beings.[3]

A BBC poll of 2000 people in the United Kingdom in 2006 showed that 'Just under half of Britons accept the theory of evolution as the best description for the development of life'.[4] A Gallup poll in the US in 2009 showed that only 39 per cent of Americans say they 'believe in the theory of evolution', while a quarter say they do not believe in the theory, and another 36 per cent don't have an opinion either way. Opinion was strongly linked to church attendance and education level, with 74 per cent of those with graduate level education expressing belief in evolution.[5] In perhaps the most subtle study of belief in evolution (J. D. Miller *et al.,* 2006), a scale of genetic literacy was included. This study included questions about whether all animals and plants had DNA and about the proportion of genes held in common between humans and chimpanzees. Unsurprisingly, the more genetically-literate people were, the more they believed in evolution. Miller and his colleagues also cite an earlier study which showed that, when presented with a description of natural selection that omitted the word evolution, 78 per cent of adults agreed to a description of the evolution of plants and animals. But 62 per cent of adults *in the same study* believed that God created humans as whole persons without any evolutionary development. It is difficult to avoid the conclusion that rejection of evolutionary thinking is often a knee-jerk reaction to *the word itself* by those without genetic understanding, rather than being a reasoned, internally consistent, position.

In a national survey of what science teachers in the USA believe, Michael Berkman and colleagues (Berkman *et al.,* 2008) outlined the history of anti-evolution advocacy in US schools. Figure 1.1 displays a summary of what science teachers believed and what a sample of the US public believed about evolution. It will be seen that far more science teachers believed in evolution (with or without

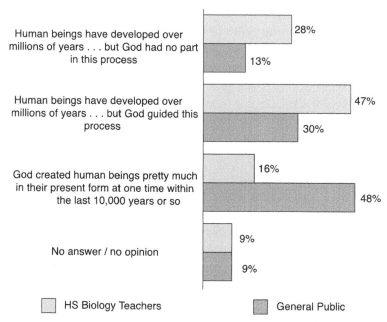

Figure 1.1 Belief about human origins: US science teachers and public (from Berkman *et al.*, 2008).

God's agency) than the public. So once again, being scientifically informed greatly increased belief in evolution. Better qualified teachers spent more class time teaching evolution. Berkman recommends that requiring all science teachers to complete a course in evolutionary biology would have a substantial impact on the emphasis on evolution and its centrality in high school biology courses.

In short, putting disparate ideas together is a very useful way of advancing knowledge; evolution is a valid and useful frame of reference, and yet substantial minorities of citizens of countries with good education systems do not accept the evolutionary account of how species emerged and changed. It therefore behoves us to summarise the evidence for evolution.

In the light of widespread disbelief, it does seem important to preface the discussion of evolution alongside crime with a brief statement of the types of evidence in support of evolution per se. Using a more recent review than that of the National Academy of Sciences cited earlier, what are the major evidence planks supporting Darwin's theory of evolution? For the moment we will restrict the discussion to the evolution of physical structure, leaving the discussion of culture in general and crime in particular until later. Jerry Coyne (2009) identifies five strong types of evidence. These are set out in Box 1.1.

Detailing examples under each category of evidence in Box 1.1 would be instructive but is beyond the scope of this book. The interested reader is referred to Jerry Coyne's excellent book referenced here, and to Richard Dawkins' more lavish book covering substantially the same material (Dawkins, 2009).

Box 1.1   'Five strong types of evidence' (Coyne, 2009)

1.   The deepest and oldest layers of rock contain the fossils of the simplest creatures, the most shallow and newest layers of rock contain the fossils of creatures which most closely resemble those living today.
2.   The fossil record, reading from oldest to most recent, yields evidence of one line of descent generating two or more different creatures.
3.   Observations in the wild demonstrate environment-driven speciation.
4.   Some species have bodies which don't work well, the imperfections only making sense in terms of evolution from other species. For example, some people have vestigial tails, and everyone has a recurrent laryngeal nerve which takes an implausibly long and unnecessarily circuitous route in people which only makes sense in the light of its location and function in our marine ancestors. Mothers can speak of the pain of childbirth, caused by human babies having acquired, through evolution, heads which are nearly too large for delivery through the pelvis.
5.   The process of natural selection is discernible in the wild.

Perhaps the most powerful statement of the position comes from the theorist Theodosius Dobzhansky:

> I venture another . . . reckless generalization. Nothing makes sense in biology except in the light of evolution. . . . If the living world has not arisen from common ancestors by means of an evolutionary process, then the fundamental unity of living things is a hoax and their diversity is a joke. The unity is understandable as a consequence of common descent and of universal necessities imposed by common materials. The diversity is intelligible as the outcome of adaptation of life to different environments.
>
> (Dobzhansky, 1964, p. 449)

The story so far: a reprise

The argument to this point contends first that criminologists have, with few exceptions, failed to bring evolutionary thinking to bear on the understanding of crime. Second, the case was made that linking disparate ideas is the essence of creative thinking, and that the evolutionary perspective has been especially fruitful in advancing understanding of phenomena other than crime. Third, it was asserted that the obstacles to teaching evolution mean that many of those entering a university education, especially in the social sciences, have only a superficial idea of the facts and implications of evolutionary theory and research. This conclusion determined the structure of the early part of this book. Our hope is that the reader leaves this chapter with a recognition that evolution provides the only compelling account of how, anatomically, species emerge and change over time. But that is only the first step on the journey. It was felt to be necessary to take that step explicitly, because of prevailing ignorance of or hostility to the underpinning theory. But extending the explanation to behaviour, and beyond that to the social construct 'crime', is a stretch, and by no means all evolutionary theorists are prepared to regard the stretch as justifiable. Evidence apart, this is scarcely surprising. Rearguard actions are still being fought by anti-evolutionists even in respect of facts that admit of no reasonable alternative explanation. Since even these facts are attacked, why make yourself vulnerable by moving on to the necessarily more speculative attempt to understand behaviour and culture? Behaviour does not leave bones and fossils, except indirectly, by way, for example, of footprints and indicators that an excavated body was that of a person who met death by human agency (like the famous iceman Otzi). Why should a scholar of the biological sciences stick her neck out to contest on ground that is not evidentially rock solid beneath her feet?

So in the next chapter we discuss how evolution works, especially in relation to levels of selection at gene, organism or group level. In Chapter 3 we contend that the very existence and scope of the criminal law is consistent with evolutionary thinking. We will outline the emotions empathy, shame and disgust, which underpin altruism and selfishness. We will conclude that sociality is key. *Homo sapiens* lacks powerful claws and teeth. The species' only prospect of prevailing against others better equipped with natural weapons lay in cooperation. This entailed the exercise of controls over errant group members. In time, such control took the form of criminal law, which formalised the contest between an errant individual and the group and which allowed the group to continue functioning in ways which minimised the waging of feuds and the pursuit of individual searches for vengeance. The criminal law will thus, it is claimed, be itself a product of the impulse to cooperate. This is arguable by the 'fit' between the behaviours proscribed by law and those that it was important to prevent in the interests of group solidarity in the ecological niche occupied at the place and time when the law was promulgated.

2 People who need people?

Introduction

The reader has (hopefully) reached this chapter prepared to accept evolution as, in the view of the overwhelming majority of scientists, the only tenable account of the wonderful structural diversity of plant and animal species on the planet which we are privileged to inhabit. If your willingness to believe this needs one last boost, consider this. Think of when you last had a course of antibiotics. Did you complete the course as you were told to? Did you do this because, if some of the troublesome bacteria which caused you to be ill survived, they would mutate and cause you to be ill again? If you answered 'yes' to all these questions and still don't believe in evolution, then we hope that with the rest of this book we make you think about organisms and crime in a different light – irrespective of whether you agree with it.

So the shaping of the structure of organisms by evolution is, scientifically, a done deal. Richard Dawkins has a reputation as an anti-religious polemicist. Yet he writes in his most recent (at the time of writing ... there will probably be another one by the time you read this) book (Dawkins, 2009) as follows:

> Bishops and theologians who have attended to the evidence for evolution have given up the struggle against it. . . . [G]rudgingly in some cases, happily in others, thoughtful and rational churchmen and women accept the evidence for evolution.
>
> (p. 6)

Suffice it to say that if God created *Homo sapiens*, She did it using a Darwinian construction manual. As Dawkins cites the former Bishop of Oxford, 'Evolution is a fact and, from a Christian perspective, one of the greatest of God's works' (p. 5).

Some of the 'thoughtful and rational churchmen and women' who accept evolution when it comes to bodies may hesitate when it comes to minds. And while evolutionary scientists can point to bones and fossils in support of Darwin, there is no Pleistocene CCTV footage available to examine hunter-gatherer behaviour. Ideas about culture and behaviour set out in this and subsequent chapters that we choose to frame in evolutionary terms could, in principle, be framed by people of a fundamentalist religious persuasion in terms of intelligent design by God. Such a reading of the facts cannot be shown to be wrong, but is not liable to evidential investigation and will not be discussed further.

Complex human interactions can be referred to in the aggregate as culture. Since we are concerned with crime, of special relevance is the shaping of behaviour which helps or harms other people, and the basis of the social arrangements which serve to encourage the former and punish the latter. The notion that how we behave is moulded in part by its survival value for our distant ancestors (LPA behaviour) may be thought demeaning. Our preferred view is that if it was so shaped, it is better to know than to remain ignorant. Acknowledging any contribution of evolution does not condemn us to a set of social arrangements, it simply clarifies how they will be opposed, how easy or difficult they will be to achieve and how best to attain or avoid them. The laissez-faire or Fascistic social policies peddled under the label of Social Darwinism are, as stressed in Chapter 1, not properly derived from evolutionary theory itself.

Charles Darwin turned his attention directly to the topic of behaviour in his last book (Darwin, 1871), in which he considered the natural selection of *instinctual* behaviour. He did original work on blushing with shame (and shame should be an interesting emotion for criminologists, reflecting as it does a discrepancy between what one does and what one thinks one should do). Reflexive behaviour like blushing can be regarded as the shallow end of the pool when it comes to persuading people of Darwin's contribution to understanding behaviour. There can be little doubt about the survival advantages of breathing, swallowing and the 'fight or flight' reaction to danger. And there has been some truly brilliant work on, for instance, the evolutionary benefits of vomiting in the early stages of pregnancy (Profet, 1992). The developing foetus is sensitive to toxins in the mother's bloodstream at levels which the mother herself could easily tolerate. Food with traces of toxins (in effect most foodstuffs) which is easily and harmlessly digested by an adult woman under normal circumstances is rejected when she becomes pregnant. As the foetus becomes less vulnerable to toxins over the course of the pregnancy, maternal sickness diminishes. But breathing, vomiting and the like are involuntary actions, a far cry from the behaviours central to culture. That said, bodies and minds are linked. People with diabetes can be irritable before insulin injections, and many other physical disorders have behavioural consequences. Let us not disrespect the reflex! Without reflexes, we would all be dead.

Of course structure and function overlap. If evolution has equipped you with a normal human brain, you can learn to speak and understand a language, pretty much any language. Allowing evolution a role in structure but not function is the most naive form of dualism. In Edward Wilson's memorable phrase (E. O. Wilson, 1978), 'genes hold culture on a leash' (p. 172). You couldn't hold a pen between thumb and finger even if you wanted to, were you to lack an opposable thumb. The nephew of one of the writers lost the thumb from his right hand in an industrial accident, and it was sad and fascinating to see what he could no longer do. Try living for an hour without using your thumbs. Please don't do this while driving, we don't want to get sued. Perhaps this nexus between structure and function is too obvious even to mention. You can't do what your body won't let you do. Your brain and body determine the range within which behaviour is possible, so any criticism that evolution applies to structure but not function has to be too simple, at best. We have already hinted that we think some criticisms of evolutionary psychology are based in part upon evolutionary biologists' determination to stand on grounds of evidence that are absolutely solid and rationally unquestionable. Engaging in more speculative work provides a hostage to fortune, a vulnerable point open to attack by those looking for a chink in the armour of the evolutionists they seek to discredit.

'Just so stories'

The best known criticism of speculative evolutionary accounts is that of Stephen Jay Gould, who described them as a series of just so stories (Gould, 1980). Gould was a hugely distinguished and respected scientist, whose criticism needs to be taken seriously. His scorn is evident.

> These speculations have been charitably called 'scenarios'; they are often more contemptuously, and rightly, labelled 'stories' (or 'just-so stories' if they rely on the fallacious assumption that everything exists for a purpose). Scientists know that these tales are stories; unfortunately, they are presented in the professional literature where they are taken too seriously and literally. Then they become 'facts' and enter the popular literature, often in such socially dubious form as the ancestral killer ape who absolves us from responsibility for our current nastiness, or as the 'innate' male dominance that justifies cultural sexism as the mark of nature.
>
> (pp. xvi–xviii)

For those not acquainted with the *Just so stories*, they were Rudyard Kipling's humorous accounts of how animals came to be as they are (Kipling, 1902). For example, the camel got his hump by magic as a punishment for being lazy (saying Humph! whenever he was asked to work), hence the appropriateness of the hump(h) as punishment; the rhinoceros got his folded skin because cake crumbs had been inserted under his skin (don't ask: read the original) and they made the rhinoceros itch so much that he scratched his skin until it developed folds. Dismissing evolution-linked speculations as just so stories is thus about as crushing a critique as it is possible to imagine. Is it fair? To some extent, it is, and readers coming across the word 'scenario' in the literature should certainly be cautious. But there is a defence.

When you have a choice between two alternatives, a and b, you can be right in two ways and wrong in two ways. You can choose a when a is correct, you can choose b when b is correct; you can choose a when b is correct, or you can choose b when a is correct. The two ways of being wrong when considering evolutionary influences on behaviour are: you can say they are there when they are not; or you can say they are not there when they are. So you can make the mistake of stating that there are evolutionary influences on behaviour when there are not, or the mistake of stating that there are not evolutionary influences on behaviour when there really are. It seems to the writers that making the latter mistake is the more pernicious, since the consequence is that we neglect the possible 'grain' of human nature, and underestimate the obstacles we face when our morality dictates that we work against it. In Edward Wilson's words (E. O. Wilson, 1994) 'Although people have free will and the choice to turn in many directions, the channels of their psychological development are . . . cut more deeply by the genes in certain directions' (pp. 332–3).

That said, we reiterate the point that evolutionary accounts can be facile, and every effort should be made to test such accounts against whatever evidence becomes available. Gould's central point is that some attributes may not be adaptations at all. Others may be attributes which come as part of a package with other traits which do enhance fitness in the Darwinian sense. A comparison can be made between evolutionary psychology and astrophysics. Both require ingenious and indirect approaches because their subject matter is distant in space or time. In astrophysics, inferences are made about the presence of planets by the wobbling and brightness changes of the stars around which they orbit. There is a 'signature' of effects. Likewise, in the best evolutionary psychology there is a search for effect signatures when considering evolutionary hypotheses about behaviour.

It's oddly reassuring that there remain many evolutionary puzzles of human nature (Barash, 2012). The reassurance comes from the ingenuity of the methods adopted to test the possibilities, and the fact that these tests have failed. Falsification is the essence of hypothetico-deductive science methods. Rigorous testing met by rejection of a hypothesis is a scientific success. If Rudyard Kipling had been a scientist wishing to establish whether his 'cake crumbs' explanation of the folds in rhinoceros skin was correct, he would have done post-mortem examinations on some animals. Struggles to explain without a facile 'explanation' indicate serious attempts to understand.

You need some examples. Same sex attraction is problematic to explain in evolutionary terms. Recent research suggests that sexual preference in a man seems to be associated with the number of older brothers he has. Each additional older brother increases the odds of a homosexual orientation by 33 per cent (Cantor *et al.*, 2002) suggesting that something in the intra-uterine environment is involved. In addition, gender preference unquestionably has a substantial heritable component (Pillard and Bailey, 1998). Both of these findings should give pause to anti-gay zealots who see sexual orientation as an unconstrained lifestyle choice. But from an evolutionary selection perspective, how can it be that gay people have not been selected out on the basis of having fewer children? The proportion of gay people is remarkably stable across cultures (Whitam, 1983).

If you have only same sex partners you will usually have few babies by the conventional route. Likewise, if you kill yourself while young, or if you have a lifestyle so criminal that you are in prison most of the time, you are likely to have fewer children than you otherwise would. Other things being equal, such behaviour should become less common. Many attempts have been made to establish an evolutionary mechanism whereby types of behaviour which curtail reproductive success are sustained.

Miller (2000) sees sexual orientation as influenced by many genes, some of which individually make for kindness and tender-mindedness. Insofar as these characteristics individually make for heterosexual mating success among men carrying them who are bisexual or predominantly heterosexual, they will be retained in the population. The speculation underpinning both of these perspectives is that gay men are particularly nurturing. Barash (2012) reviews evidence casting doubt on this assumption. Back to the drawing board? Attempting to understand homosexuality in evolutionary terms remains a work in progress. Perhaps so. It doesn't matter. The approach shows that falsification is possible. The science is better than just so stories.

The evidence base for evolutionary psychology has to be distinctive. So the approach is typically to look at the ways in which people behave, see what makes sense in evolutionary terms, and make testable predictions about other areas of behaviour which are inconsistent with the hypothesised explanation. Sometimes known as retrodiction, this approach ideally yields a picture which makes sense only in the light of the theory in question. The human tendency to seek confirmation rather than falsification is our enemy here. The ideal is to design studies where certain outcomes would show that one is wrong.

How evolution might work

There are some crime-related examples of the process of retrodiction to which we will come in due course. Before we discuss these, we have to give a more detailed account of how evolution might work, particularly about precisely how natural selection can be thought of. This is necessary because we need to explore how helpful or exploitative behaviour towards other people might confer a selection advantage.

A full description of the debates about what constitutes evidence in evolutionary accounts is beyond the scope of this book. The issue requires a volume in itself. Fortunately, such a book already exists, entitled *Sense and nonsense: evolutionary perspectives on human behaviour* (Laland and Brown, 2002). The title suggests that the text will be direct and clear, and possibly combative, and it does not disappoint. It seeks to assess the methods of research brought to bear to sustain claims about human nature made under the name of evolution. Laland and Brown distinguish five approaches: human sociobiology, human behavioural ecology, evolutionary psychology, memetics and gene-culture co-evolution. Each has distinctive features, whether of method of hypothesis generation, comparisons entailed or the adaptive status of attributes focused on. The book is strongly recommended to readers wanting an in-depth treatment of approaches to evolutionary theory. Its final chapter provides a tentative integration of the five theoretic approaches which the book's authors identify.

Working out its implications is complex, but the core of Darwinian theory is extraordinarily simple, as we hope you demonstrated by visiting Darwintunes as recommended in Chapter 1. To restate, individuals within a species vary. Those variants which succeed in their specific environment (i.e. have more offspring surviving to reproduce) will, over the course of generations, come to predominate numerically. This does not mean that they will completely take over. Predator species will vary in numbers depending on the size of the prey population. When prey is scarce, predator numbers will decline. Prey species will vary in numbers depending on the size of the predator population. When predators are numerous, the size of the prey population will decline (which then triggers a decline in predator population, and so on). *Within* a species, the same dynamic applies. For example, individuals who are tolerant of a wider range of plants on which to feed will increase in numbers during hard times. Specialist feeders will increase when their primary food supply is large. We will return to this issue when we discuss human 'free-riders', i.e. people who behave selfishly in a generally cooperative group.

Because it is essentially so simple, Darwinian theory can be applied at a range of levels. First, it may be helpful to distinguish replicators and survival vehicles. Replicators are the things/organisms/skills/ideas whose numbers are destined to increase or decrease. Survival vehicles are the means they use to do so. If one considers *genes* as replicators, *organisms* are the survival vehicles. This was the central insight of Richard Dawkins' best-selling book *The selfish gene*. Those genes which incline the organism to act in ways which ensure its (and thus their) survival will increase in number. On this perspective, a person is just a gene's way of making more genes. If one now considers *organisms* as replicators, the *cooperative group* is the means which they use to ensure survival. So the cooperative group is the person's way of making more people. Take a breath. If one considers *ideas* or *skills* as replicators, the *culture* is the survival vehicle. So the culture is the skill's way of making more skills. One can think of a whole range of replicators and their associated survival vehicles. A half-remembered quote is that people are a library's way of making more libraries. Look at the successive generations of Apple iPhones. Successful features and apps survive and are refined, others disappear. iPhones are the *replicator*, people the *survival vehicle*. Applying the simple core imaginatively mines a rich vein of theory, not so far applied to crime and criminality to any appreciable extent. This is one of the reasons why the writers think evolutionary thinking has rich promise for criminology, as for other social sciences – and perhaps for designers and engineers, by the use of evolutionary algorithms (EA). The process is precisely the same as you experienced in Darwintunes. EAs take (say) two parent designs (for a racing car, for example) and blend components to produce multiple 'offspring'. Then a selection process (say drag measurement in a wind tunnel) selects the designs worth 're-breeding'. The process is then repeated over many generations. Useful features thereby accumulate in the same design, and get combined in ways that may not have occurred to a human designer because a human does not have the time to combine all the possibilities and evaluate them, but an EA does. Googling 'evolutionary algorithms' will give you an idea of how such an approach is coming to permeate design thinking.

There is very little in this book about genetics. Chapter 8 is as close as we get, and then only because we think the strand of research which we describe there will loom large in many contexts, from cancer treatment to human stress reduction. Readers may be surprised by the absence of genetics elsewhere in the book. There are at least three reasons for this. First, Darwin did not have access to modern genetic knowledge and did not need it (although he would certainly have been pleased and overwhelmed that the discipline vindicated and advanced his work so much). The mechanisms of genetic transmission have added hugely to our understanding of genetic drift, genetic bottlenecks when populations were small, and periods when there were fast changes in the genome because of selection pressure. But an understanding of evolution, while enriched by appreciating its genetic undergirding, is entirely possible without it. Second, as noted above, there are ways of thinking about evolution in relation to skills and ideas (known collectively as memes) which are not about genes at all, and an undue emphasis on genetics might downplay their importance. Third, recent years have shown how provisional is our understanding of gene function. Two weeks before writing this, the ENCODE project[1] astonished the science community by showing that a huge proportion of the human genome (which was previously disparagingly referred to as 'junk DNA' because it did not code for proteins) in fact comprised gene *switches*. These determine which protein-coding genes are functional, and which are disabled. Since the ideas behind evolution can stand apart from this work, and since discussion of the relevant research would certainly be outdated by the time you pick up this book, it seemed better not to major on evolution-relevant genetic research (except for Chapter 8, as noted).

Eusociality

Ants and termites have it. We have it. What is it? Eusociality is the condition in which *multiple generations* are organised into *groups* characterised by *division of labour* (E. O. Wilson, 2012). Language is an important enabling technology to make such social arrangements work. Eusociality seems successful in that, Wilson asserts, 'animals of the land environment are dominated by species with the most complex social systems' (p. 109). Wilson is intrigued that, given its success, eusociality has not evolved more often. He observes three principles of eusocial living:

1   All species which have attained eusociability live in fortified sites;
2   The protection afforded is against predators, parasites and competitors;
3   Even small societies do better than a solitary individual in closely related species, in longevity and the extraction of resources.

The third principle is crucial in considering evolved inclinations to behave in particular ways, what we have described above as the grain of human nature, a metaphor relating to wood, which is worked most easily along rather than against the grain. According to Edward Wilson, we acquired eusociality in a fundamentally different way from ants and termites, and we have tried to avoid species comparisons as far as possible because of the predictable 'people and termites are different' knee-jerk reaction to such comparisons. That said, it's interesting how often researchers studying ants and termites see parallels with human social organisation. For example, Moffett (2011) writes

> Scientists have long known that certain kinds of ants (and termites) form tight-knit societies with members numbering in the millions and that these insects engage in complex behaviours. Such practices include traffic management, public health efforts, crop domestication and, perhaps most intriguingly, warfare: the concentrated engagement of group against group in which both sides risk wholesale destruction. Indeed, in these respects and others, we modern humans more closely resemble ants than our closest living relatives, the apes, which live in far smaller societies.
>
> (p. 86)

The topic of convergent evolution, whereby the same attribute is acquired by different routes (see, for example, Emery and Clayton, 2004), is beyond the modest scope of this book. Nonetheless it is worth mentioning in passing, since it is common and is another evidence source in support of evolution theory.

Among mammals, human social arrangements are by a very wide margin the most complex, disparate and ubiquitous. The word disparate is crucial because of the improper equation of biological with uniform or unchanging. There is uniformity only in the generality of kinds of social behaviour which one finds across human settlements, the so-called cross-cultural universals (see Box 2.1).

Box 2.1   The 67 social arrangements shared by all societies: an alphabetic listing from the Human Relations Area Files (Murdock, 1945)

Age-grading, athletic sports, bodily adornment, botany, calendar, cleanliness training, community organisation, cooking, cooperative labour, cosmology, courtship, dancing, decorative art, divination, division of labour, dream interpretation, education, eschatology, ethics, etiquette, faith healing, family feasting, fire-making, folklore, food taboos, funeral rites, games, gestures, gift-giving, government, greetings, hair styles, hospitality, housing, hygiene, incest taboos, inheritance rules, joking, kin groups, kinship nomenclature, language, law, luck superstitions, magic, marriage, mealtimes, medicine, obstetrics, penal sanctions, personal names, population policy, post-natal care, pregnancy usages, property rights, propitiation of supernatural beings, puberty customs, religious ritual, residence rules, sexual restrictions, soul concepts, status differentiation, surgery tool-making, trade, visiting, weather control and weaving.

For example, funeral rites are ubiquitous, but the specifics of those rites vary, encompassing a wide range of practices.

The common denominator of cultures

Box 2.1 shows an alphabetic listing of the 67 social arrangements shared by all the societies on which information was available in the database the Human Relations Area Files, as gleaned by George Murdock in his classic study (Murdock, 1945). No doubt caution should be exercised in accepting this list. It is included because it demonstrates that many complex social forms are widespread or ubiquitous in human settlements.

So we have eusociality. Put the word aside and just try to think as a visitor from Mars. Surely the aspect of *Homo sapiens* that it (assuming Martians are asexual) would find most remarkable would be the lust for company and communication, for living and doing things together rather than alone. In prisons, solitary confinement is a punishment rather than a privilege. The mushroom growth of social networking might astonish our Martian visitor. People, having spent a day at school, college or work interacting with others, come home and choose to interact digitally! We seem designed to favour group communication and collaboration.

Levels of selection

The 'levels of selection' controversy involves a range of disciplines, from philosophy to population genetics. For a scholarly and technical exploration of the topic, see Okasha (2006). The discussion here is limited to what might be helpful to the reader as a preamble to the discussion of criminal law and criminality.

We touched on this topic when we discussed replicators and survival vehicles. You are a person. You comprise a set of organs: heart, liver, spleen, etc. Each of those organs comprises cells. The nucleus of each cell in each of those organs contains a number of chromosomes. Each of those chromosomes contains many genes. Each gene contains . . . there's no need to go further. So, working inwards from the person unit, there is a series of 'nested' levels at which one can theorise. Returning to the perspective of the whole organism (you), looking outwards, you are a member of a family, a group of people you know well, you live in a street, and perhaps belong to work, religious and hobby groups.[2] You have a nationality and belong to a species which is part of a clade.[3]

To paraphrase Darwin, if a population leaves more offspring which themselves reproduce (i.e. fitness), and if the offspring resemble their parents, over time the population will change, the fitter variants coming to predominate. But what is the population a population of? The common sense way is to think of the population as a population of individual people, but it is just as easy to think (looking inwards) of the population as a population of *genes* or (looking outwards) as a population of *groups* of humans, tribes or whatever.

Let us take an example of interesting group dynamics. There seems to be a limit to the size of your face-to-face social group (thus excluding 'friendship' groups on social networking sites like Facebook and Twitter). The 'Dunbar number' refers to the maximum number of other people with whom a person can maintain stable social relationships (R. I. M. Dunbar, 1992). Robin Dunbar found a relatively narrow band of group sizes with an average of 150. This number (plus or minus some) characterised group size among numerous contemporary hunter-gatherer groups, and the average estimated size of Neolithic farming villages. Modern comparisons were made with the size of military units. So there are limits to the size of truly interacting groups. The evolutionary connection is that Dunbar linked neocortex size as the factor which limits group size among primates. Does the Dunbar number of itself suggest group level selection? It does not. If limited food availability at the time made mortality rates in larger settlements high, and/ or smaller settlements found it difficult to muster hunting parties large enough to kill the available prey while leaving enough people to protect the settlement against marauders (also leading to high mortality and group extinction or combination), such accounts could perhaps be interpreted as group level selection. Dunbar links modal human group size to brain development, so possibly the anticipation that hunting range was becoming insufficient to sustain group numbers might lead to an agreed group division (an individual level explanation). Perhaps people varied then (as they do now) at the gene level in their tolerance of crowds, so splinter groups of those most averse to crowds left when settlements got too crowded; that would be a gene level selection. All these possibilities are speculative, but are included to show that the Dunbar number, like other phenomena of the same kind, does not lead inexorably to one or other level of selection being preferred.

Whatever its evolutionary origins, the Dunbar number has major unexplored implications for designing conflict-minimal contemporary human settlements. We already know that certain street types are associated with low levels of crime (Johnson and Bowers, 2010) and, at worst, using an evolutionary approach to the dynamics which make this so would be interesting, but it is a temptation we must resist here. To restate the essential point, one can think of a series of levels, working inwards and outwards from the person, at which natural selection can work. But does the existence of the Dunbar number suggest that selection occurs at least in part at the group level? It does not.

Does it matter which level of selection is chosen for analysis, since by and large evolution tends to move in the same direction whichever level of selection one chooses? It does matter, especially for a discussion of pro-social and anti-social behaviour, because *sometimes* what is good for the gene is not good for the organism, and what is good for the organism is not good for the family or tribe. To take an example, parasitic diseases that do not kill you are good for the parasites but not good for you.[4] Even cancer can be thought of as good (until the host dies) for the proliferation of cancer cells, but not good for the body it takes over. The issue which leads us on to the topic of crime is altruism and its converse, self-centredness. If heroes die, their heroic genes die with them. If the self-centred flourish, they inherit the Earth, rather than the meek (apologies to the meek for any disappointment).

We start life being horribly selfish. Birth weight of the foetus is not substantially influenced by the protein value of the diet consumed by the mother during pregnancy.

> Only when severe and prolonged malnutrition is experienced before conception is obstetrical performance impaired. . . . It may be concluded, therefore, that on a low plane of nutrition, the foetus lives as a parasite, the tissues of the foetus having a prior claim on the nutrients circulating in the maternal blood stream.
>
> (Naismith, 1969, p. 25)

But most people go on, in varying degrees, to be altruistic: to do people favours, to give to charity, and even to sacrifice their lives to a collective cause. Altruism is the behavioural phenomenon which has most exercised evolutionary scientists. This makes it the same sort of problem as homosexuality and elective vasectomy. If altruists die in the course of being helpful, why haven't altruists ceased to exist?

On a lighter (but linked) note, we point the reader towards the annual Darwin Awards. The awards 'salute the improvement of the human genome by honoring those who accidentally remove themselves from it'.

The awards are mostly about acts of unbelievable stupidity. Take, for example, a 1996 winner:

> Krystof Azninski staked a strong claim to being Europe's most macho man by cutting off his own head in 1995. Azninski, 30, had been drinking with friends when it was suggested they strip naked and play some 'men's games'. Initially they hit each other over the head with frozen turnips, but then one man upped the ante by seizing a chainsaw and cutting off the end of his foot. Not to be outdone, Azninski grabbed the saw and, shouting 'Watch this then,' he swung at his own head and chopped it off.[5]

But why don't altruists who die in the course of their heroism ever receive the Darwin Award? They are removing themselves from the human genome as effectively as the self-decapitator.

Darwin himself recognised altruism as a central problem for evolution *at the level of the individual organism*. He mused about the evolution of sterility in insects such as worker bees (Darwin, 1859). Worker bees devote themselves to activities which serve the interests of the hive as a whole, at the expense of their own well-being. He extended his speculation to humans: 'A tribe including many members who . . . were always ready to give aid to each other and sacrifice themselves for the common good, would be victorious over most other tribes and this would be natural selection'(Darwin, 1871, p. 166).

Darwin did not have the benefit of knowing about modern genetics. The brilliant W. D. Hamilton did (Hamilton, 1963). His altruism argument was couched at the gene level. You share half your genes with your siblings. If you risk your life saving two siblings (and it is not certain that you will die in the attempt) altruism makes sense. If you have an identical twin, it should be a matter of indifference which of the two of you die, if either has to. Kin selection makes sense in explaining altruistic behaviour towards relatives. Indeed, even sharing the same name increases altruism, since it serves as a suggestion of kinship. Shared rare names are especially potent at eliciting altruism, since they are more likely to reflect kinship (Oates and Wilson, 2002). Altruism advances group interests. The worker bee which stings and dies helps repel hive predators. Since each worker bee is a twin sister of every other worker bee in the hive, her sacrifice advances the interests of her sisters. So at the gene level, saving one identical twin (and a bit) is worth the death of the stinger. Altruistic expendability can be very subtle:

> Old-aged termites go out with a bang, it appears. While ageing, the insects brew a backpack of deadly chemicals, which they use to self-destruct when under attack, taking out any enemies with them. . . . When the spotted termites were physically unable to defend themselves with their jaws, they would commit the ultimate sacrifice and burst a pouch on their backs, releasing a toxic liquid that quickly paralysed and killed any other termites it touched
>
> (Griggs, 2012, p. 14)

Making too crude a jump to *Homo sapiens*, a father shares 50 per cent of his genes with each of his children. Sacrificing himself so that more than two of his children survive is advantageous at the gene level.[6] Altruistic behaviour which serves the interests of one's relatives can thus be consistent with natural selection at the level of the gene. *Inclusive fitness* is the term used when taking this wider view. If your sacrifice of yourself means that more of your genes survive vicariously, in the bodies of your relatives, than would otherwise be the case, we introduce the notion of *kin selection*. We will encounter kin selection later in the book as part of the discussion of infanticide.

We earlier discussed the problem that homosexuality presents for evolutionary explanation, and attempts to answer it have mostly rested on two kinds of thinking, one of which concerns kin selection. If gay people offer more support to their parents in the rearing of their brothers and sisters, leading to the survival to adulthood of more of the siblings, homosexual preference would be selected for by dint of the genes shared between the gay family member and his or her siblings (E. O. Wilson, 1978). A similar account has been attempted of the menopause, whereby a grandmother's contribution to the survival chances of her grandchildren more than offsets the loss incurred by having no more children of her own (Sear *et al.*, 2000).

The remaining and fundamental problem is that people are not only altruistic towards relatives. So we need to think about levels of selection for a while. One approach to explaining altruism to those not related, and by the way illustrating a possible means of group level selection, is to distinguish strong and weak altruism (Sober and Wilson, 1998). In strong altruism, the benefit to the group is bought at an absolute cost to the actor. Strong altruism can only spread if 'birds of a feather flock together', i.e. if people tend to form groups with people of the same type, so that altruistic behaviour helps other altruists. The notion of selection by reputation is a relative newcomer to the scene. A good reputation can be converted (Pagel, 2012) into money, acceptance and sexual success. When you buy something on eBay, do you look at the seller's reputation box in the top right of the screen before deciding whether to go ahead? The grotesque extreme of the importance of reputation is the honour killing. There is experimental work to show how the two poles of reputation (shame and honour) can, without any extrinsic reward, drive cooperation (Jacquet *et al.*, 2011). And the guiltiest people are the people with the least to feel guilty about (Cohen *et al.*, 2012).

The researchers tested this hypothesis with anonymous six-player games in which generosity could be measured. They instructed the players that the two individuals who were least generous, and those who were most generous after ten rounds, would be exposed to the group.

> The non-monetary, reputational effects induced by shame and honour each led to approximately 50 per cent higher donations to the public good when compared with the control, demonstrating that both shame and honour can drive cooperation and can help alleviate the tragedy of the commons.[7]
>
> (p. 899)

> Here is a profoundly uncomfortable illustration of both the power of (perceived) reputation in human society ... [W]e are willing to kill our offspring to pay off the reputation debt of their perceived transgression and therefore keep our own reputation intact.
>
> (p. 224–225)

The honour killing is the disgusting downside of the reputation market. In more defensible terms, insistence on reputation picks out people whom one can trust to uphold common standards and thus bring strong altruism into play. As noted above, for strong altruism to work, you need a flag to indicate people who are like you. This was labelled by Richard Dawkins the 'green beard' effect (Dawkins, 1976).

A green beard effect occurs when a gene, or genes, yield

1   a discernible and recognised trait (the green beard);
2   preferential treatment to people with the trait.

So much for strong altruism. In weak altruism, the selfless behaviour may not advantage the actor at all or may advantage the actor but to a lesser extent than it advances the interests of other members of the group. Under these circumstances, weak altruism can increase in frequency over generations. Of course, the calculation of advantage in everyday life is a complex matter. One insight is that selfless behaviour can work to one's advantage if there is a continuing relationship with the recipient of altruism. In groups that are stable over time and where the memory of previous encounters endures, altruism to non-relatives can be the best way to go. This reciprocal altruism (Trivers, 1971) results in trust. Perhaps this is why the Dunbar number limits the size of functioning groups. Two contributions by scholars coincidentally called Wilson alert us to how group level selection might work. David Sloan Wilson's trait group model (D. S. Wilson, 1975) is the first. To simplify, let us term people as altruists and predators (not Wilson's term). They live in groups. *Within* each group, predators have higher fitness than altruists (i.e. they have more children surviving to reproductive age). However, groups containing more altruists cooperate more and in consequence have a higher *group* fitness, and so contribute more individuals to the global population. The second contribution comes from Edward O. Wilson, a scholar as controversial as he is distinguished. In his espousal of group level selection in his latest book (E. O. Wilson, 2012) he writes

> A group with members who could read intentions and cooperate . . . would have an enormous advantage over others less gifted. There was undoubtedly competition among group members, leading to natural selection of traits that gave advantage to one individual over another. But more important for a species entering new environments and competing with powerful rivals were unity and cooperation within the group.
>
> (p. 224)

Even more succinctly, he proposes an 'iron rule' in genetic social evolution. It is that 'selfish individuals beat altruistic individuals, while groups of altruists beat groups of selfish individuals' (p. 243).

Although neither law nor crime appear in the index to Wilson's book, these concepts fit neatly into the Wilson world-view, in which the cohesion of social groupings is secured by the (imperfect) glue of individual altruism, against the backcloth of the within-group success of the selfish.

So evolution divides us into cooperators (the majority) and freeloaders (the minority). What do we do about the freeloaders? One approach would be to do nothing. A drawback of such a policy is that it might lead to a large increase in criminal activity, which might then be hard to reduce. We do not venture into the topic, which gets into complex econometrics quite quickly (Gordon *et al.*, 2009). What is clear from observation is that communities comprising mostly freeloaders are very bad news (N. Ross and Pease, 2008). The conditions for altruism are precarious, and you will be aware of extreme differences in risk and disorder in your own town or city.

We should end with brief mention of the work of Martin Nowak and collaborators, who approached the group selection issue with an entirely different approach, that of the mathematical modelling of the Prisoner's Dilemma game (Nowak, 2011). His conclusion about selection at the group level overlaps with what has been written above, but goes a little further. His work yields five group attributes which make for the success of cooperative groups over competitive groups. These are as follows:

1   *Direct reciprocity*: 'Overall, direct reciprocity can lead to the evolution of cooperation only if the probability of another encounter between the same two individuals exceeds the cost-to-benefit ratio of the altruistic act' (p. 270).

2   *Indirect reciprocity*: this 'can only promote cooperation if the probability of knowing someone's reputation exceeds the cost-to-benefit ratio of the altruistic act' (p. 271)

3   *Spatial selection*: 'co-operators can prevail by forming networks and clusters in which they help each other more often than others. . . . The benefit-to-cost ratio must exceed the number of neighbours per individual' (p. 271).

4   *Multilevel selection*: works if 'the ratio of the benefits to cost is greater than one plus the ratio of group size to number of groups. Thus this cooperative mechanism works well if there are many small groups and not too well if there are a few large groups' (p. 271)

5   *Kin selection*: the degree of 'relatedness must exceed the cost-to-benefit ratio of the altruistic act' (p. 272).

Perhaps special attention should be drawn to the conclusion about spatial selection. The *clustering* of cooperators in small groups is necessary. In the world outside the laboratory, people can move to join more cooperative groups in more congenial areas. This is important for thinking about the huge area disparity in crime rates.

Reprise and next steps

The chapter has rehearsed ideas about how an evolutionary perspective can advance understanding of the complex human interactions we refer to in the aggregate as culture. It discussed natural selection and the kinds of behaviour it has problems in explaining, especially altruism. It presented kin selection and inclusive fitness as partial answers to understanding altruism. It sought to illustrate how groups which endure over time and where interactions between individuals are remembered can confer selection advantage to altruistic behaviour. It described the position of E. O. Wilson and the work of Martin Nowak in contending that group level selection results in a state of affairs where within-group advantage may go to the selfish but groups with higher proportions of altruists will prevail at the group level.

You may think this chapter was unduly academic because the circumstances which shaped the behaviour described may no longer apply. The residents of your street are (hopefully) not going to get wiped out if you fail to join the battle against those engaging in anti-social behaviour there, or if you decline to join the local Neighbourhood Watch. But your emotions and predispositions may have been formed in an era when altruism and cooperation were sometimes a matter of life and death, either directly by aggression or indirectly by reducing the numbers of those born in troubled groups, and the same emotions and predispositions remain relevant today. They were Late Pleistocene Appropriate (LPA) and we are saddled with them. After all, it is as important to explain why most do not commit crime as it is to explain why some do. This is something that criminology often neglects.

In the next chapter we consider the feeling side of altruism, empathy, the evolutionary implications of having a criminal law at all, and the crimes that people commit on which evolutionary thinking throws a light.

3 Theory of Mind, empathy and criminal behaviour

Introduction

We hope the reader comes to this chapter persuaded that the sociability of people in general is spectacularly great, and that evolution made that important for group survival. Language, and the fact that criminal law exists at all, is testament to the unique sociability of *Homo sapiens* amongst mammals. To reiterate, the position of many students of evolution and culture is that

- Cooperating human groups will enjoy more reproductive success than groups of selfish people;
- *within* human groups, a selfish individual is likely to enjoy the advantage;
- these two facts create a tension within groups which criminal law is designed to moderate.

But if most of us are disposed to cooperate, and you are one of 'most of us', we ought to be able to point to your own experience for evidence. After all, if we are right, evolutionary legacy is reflected in *your* preferences and inclinations. What is the cognitive and emotional underpinning of the urge to sociability which eventually gave us criminal law? What do *you* think and feel that leads you to cooperate and display at least weak altruism in your dealings with other people? You need three things:

1 The recognition that other people have thoughts and emotions similar to yours, i.e. *a theory of mind*;
2 The capacity to feel with other people, i.e. *empathy*; and
3 An emergent idea of fairness, however warped; i.e. *a sense of justice*.

Let us take these things in order. We will deal with the first two in this chapter, and the sense of justice in Chapter 4.

Theory of Mind (ToM)

French philosopher and mathematician René Descartes decided to doubt his own existence, in a work originally published in 1637 but referenced here in translation

(Descartes, 1960). He concluded that, as *somebody* was doing the doubting (i.e. him) then he must exist, proclaiming famously, 'I think therefore I am'. Most of us go a step further, and think that others think. Writing this, we think you think. We try to think how you think, and we try to shape this text so that it meshes with your thought processes. This means we have a theory of mind (Premack and Woodruff, 1978).

Chapter 2 described how humans, as a species, evolved to be ultra-social animals. We constructed a complex 'social world' for ourselves to inhabit and, uniquely, languages capable of describing things not present and negotiating collaborations not yet undertaken. Why are we capable of putting ourselves in the place of others?

> Presumably, the ability to better predict other people's behaviour from knowledge of their beliefs and desires helped early humans to solve adaptive problems such as anticipating hostile attacks, enlisting aid from those who might be inclined to give it, pacifying conflicting parents, making threats more credible, forming coalitions, and so forth.
>
> (Buss, 2004, p. 390)

Theory of Mind is arguably the best known and most studied of all human social cognition mechanisms. It is meant to suggest that the individual has a testable belief (a theory) about the content of (another person's) mind – in other words, he/she understands that other people have mental states (thoughts, desires, beliefs) and that these mental states drive their behaviour. More importantly, perhaps, the individual can appreciate that, at any time, the actual content of these mental states can differ considerably from our own and from the objective reality of a situation (Barrett *et al.*, 2002, p. 296–7). You should not need persuading that you have a theory of mind. If you do, and you have a pet, think of how often you project thoughts and feelings on to the pet, and arrange the environment so that its false beliefs are remedied. (You thought your ball was over there. I moved it. Here it is.) Scientists sniffily call this anthropomorphism, but really it shows that you have a theory of mind which extends to loved animals, and perhaps animals generally.

How can you tell whether someone has a theory of mind? Some really ingenious research has gone into establishing when a theory of mind develops, and because it is central to our theme, we will describe it briefly. The key to establishing whether someone has a theory of mind lies in finding out whether they can detect the *false beliefs* of others. Wimmer and Perner found that children begin correctly to predict mistaken actions based on a false belief around the age of four years (Wimmer and Perner, 1983). The classic experiment goes like this. A doll called Maxi is shown to the child. The child is told that Maxi keeps his chocolate bar in a green cupboard. Maxi is then removed from the scene (the child is told that Maxi is 'going to the playground'). Another doll ('Maxi's mother') enters. She wants to bake a cake. She takes Maxi's chocolate out of the green cupboard, breaks off a piece and puts the remaining chocolate in the *blue* cupboard. Maxi returns and his mother goes away again. The child has to answer several questions. The key question concerns where Maxi will search for his chocolate. Three-year-olds generally mistakenly guess the *blue* cupboard. This is because they think Maxi will know what the child knows, neglecting the fact that the chocolate was moved to the blue cupboard in Maxi's absence. However, up to 80 per cent of 4–5-year-olds answer correctly that Maxi will search for the chocolate in the, *green* cupboard. So by the age of five, most children recognise that the beliefs and perspectives of someone else differ from their own. More subtle social inferences of the kind in which we are interested come later (Pillow, 1991). The stage of development at which the theory of mind kicks in has been found to be roughly constant across cultures (Avis and Harris, 1991).

Do other species have a theory of mind? In a famous study by Premack and Woodruff (1978), Sarah the chimpanzee was shown films of human actors facing various problems. In one, the actor was in a situation where he was struggling to get some bananas hanging over his head but just out of reach. Sarah, after watching the film, was shown three photographs depicting different actions for solving the problem, but only one represented a good solution (stepping on a chair). Sarah chose the 'correct' answer well above chance levels, the researchers concluding that she demonstrated an ability to understand what the actor's intentions were (i.e. to reach the bananas). Where strict behaviourist psychologists might dismiss this claim as simply 'conditioning', other psychologists might call this having a Theory of Mind (Premack and Woodruff, 1978).

One of us had a pet cat who would come and find us and start miaowing the minute the microwave oven 'pinged' at the end of defrosting his fish supper. He did not, however, miaow every time the microwave pinged, just when it was defrosting his fish. Did this cat have a theory of mind or was he just good at smelling fish being cooked, or telling the time? If we were searching for his fish in the wrong place and he beckoned us over to the right place, then we might have concluded that he was a ToM cat (sorry). Until experiments are devised which are viable for non-human animals and which, crucially, induce a false belief in one of the participants, the question remains open.

So by the age of four, dear reader, you almost certainly had taken possession of a theory of mind of your very own. How have you used it? You could have used it to collaborate with people or to outwit them. If you are reading this in prison, or are a banker on your yacht, you probably did the latter. Having a theory of mind, in a world which favours cooperative groups (see Chapter 2) is necessary but not sufficient to understand our generally pro-social behaviour. We need something extra which inclines us to be kind, to trust and to cooperate generally, and something that inclines us to punish selectively when the trust is betrayed. We need something which explains the immediate reaction of Jack, the four-year-old grandson of one of the writers. His mother is a mental health lawyer. While heavily pregnant with her second child, she visited a secure hospital to see a client. Care had to be taken because one female patient had been known to attack pregnant visitors. Talking about the visit later at home, Jack speculated that the poor woman had wanted children of her own but was unable to have them. This beautifully illustrates that Jack had fully acquired his theory of mind, *and* that his standing decision was kindly and sociable. Enter empathy.

Empathy

This is a book about evolution and crime, so the key issue to be addressed is how might the three conditions, a theory of mind, empathy and a sense of fairness have developed in the first place? What was in it for our forebears? How is it most fruitful to think about empathy? Box 3.1 provides a stunning example of an altruism deficit. It is genuine.[1]

Jean Decety suggests that the 'human social brain' is built upon the same foundations as that of other animals. Put more eloquently, those foundations are 'ancient emotional and motivational value systems that generate affective states as indicators of potential fitness trajectories' (2011, p. 36). The origin of human empathy is likely to be the impulse to nurture offspring, one manifestation of the kin selection – inclusive fitness notions that we discussed in a previous chapter. So why do we have the capacity to empathise with people to whom we are not related, like those we do not know or those we are never likely to meet? The explanation we favoured earlier was that weak altruism (at least) pays off if it forms part of enduring relationships, with the development of trust and the expectation that altruism displayed will be altruism returned at some future date. To fix the idea in your mind, we cannot resist citing the case of vampire bats. Vampire bats die if they fail to feed for two nights in a row. Bats that have done

---

Box 3.1   Letter from a burglar to their victim

Our thanks to West Yorkshire Police for the following letter

Dear victim

I dont no Why Iam writing a letter to you! I haVe been forced to Write this letter by ISSp. TO be honest I'm not bothered or Sorry about the fact that I burgled your houSe. Basicly it Was your fault anyways. I'm going to run you through the dumb mistakes you made. firstly you didnt draw your curtainS Which moSt people now to do before they go to Sleep. Secondly your dumb you liVe in Stainburns a high risk burglary area and your thick enough to leave your b downstairs kitchen Window open. I Wouldnt do that in a million years. But anyways I dont feel Sorry for you and Im not going to show any sympath or ~~remose~~ remores.

YourS Sincerly

Note: The original handwriting is difficult to reproduce so this typeset version is to facilitate the reader's understanding.

---

well in their hunt and are full of blood will regurgitate some to their less fortunate colleagues (Wilkinson, 1984, Wilkinson, 1988). A video clip of the process is available, with the first comment posted being 'who would have thought vampire bats have morals?'[2]

As for altruism towards unknown people (and vampire bats to each other), we discussed that in terms of the reputation economy. Being seen as a good person by the recipient of favours *and onlookers* has reputation benefits that can be 'cashed in' later in the currency of willingness to deal with you.

Empathy without a theory of mind is impossible. To have empathy with someone you have to recognise them as being like you in having beliefs, knowledge, desires and goals, although those emotions and aspirations may be different from yours. You have to recognise that their emotions when disappointed or hurt are similar to those you experience when you yourself are disappointed or hurt. Obviously empathy has both cognitive and emotional elements. We have all met people who just seem not to notice the misery of others but are kind once they do notice.

What do you call a person with high empathy? A sociopath would call her a sucker. A *Star Trek* fan would call her an empath, and so shall we, in an attempt to rescue this nice short word from the bad company into which it has fallen. In *Star Trek* Episode 12 of Season 3, an alien called Gem (the empath) absorbs the pain of others, so that she suffers *instead of them*. In *Star Trek: The Next Generation* the empath Deanna Troi uses her *telepathic* gifts in various ways throughout the series. This *Star Trek* mystical view of empaths is the one that caught on. You can check this assertion by Googling the word. Most sites listed put the *Star Trek mystical* spin on the word, for example claiming that empaths 'have the ability to scan another's psyche for thoughts and feelings or for past, present, and future life occurrences'.[3] They are 'the psychic sponges of the universe, absorbing the emotions and psychic pollution that is around them'.[4] It is interesting that the *Star Trek* empaths are both female, and we will touch on the question of gender and empathy later.

Empaths in the real world, cognitively aware and responding emotionally to the feelings of others, are miraculous enough. We should eschew the *Star Trek* inspired psychobabble surrounding the term and reclaim it for proper use. We are nearly all, to varying degrees, empaths.

> The experience of empathy is a powerful interpersonal phenomenon and a necessary means of everyday social communication. It facilitates parental care of offspring. It enables us to live in groups and to socialize. It paves the way for the development of moral reasoning and motivates prosocial altruistic behaviour.
>
> (Decety, 2011, p. 35)

The philosopher Michael Slote suggests that up until the early twentieth century the term 'sympathy' was considered expansive enough to include what we now refer to as 'empathy' (Slote, 2011). The difference between sympathy and empathy, although perhaps subtle to some, is important none the less. For example, the Rolling Stones song *Sympathy for the Devil* would be a much less palatable lyric for many had it been called 'Empathy for the Devil' instead. Why? Here is a good attempt to illustrate the difference between them: 'For most of us today, empathy differs from sympathy in the way that 'I feel your pain' (empathy) differs from 'I feel sorry about your being in pain' (sympathy)' (Slote, 2011, p. 13).

In the beginning of his wonderful book on the subject, *Zero degrees of empathy*, the psychologist Simon Baron-Cohen takes time to explore how empathy might best be defined. He begins by suggesting that empathy is when we adopt a double-minded focus of attention (Baron-Cohen, 2011). Empaths empathise when they pay attention to other people's minds (i.e. their thoughts and feelings) at the same time as paying attention to their own. Similarly, Zinn describes empathy from a medical practitioner's perspective as 'the intellectual identification with, or vicarious experiencing of the feelings, thoughts, or attitudes of another; the imaginative ascribing to an object, as a natural object or work of art, feelings, or attitudes present in oneself' (Zinn, 1993, p. 306).

Baron-Cohen suggests that any definition (including his) is incomplete if it does not include the 'process and content' of what is happening when we empathise. He offers the following further more comprehensive definition: 'Empathy is our ability to identify what someone else is thinking or feeling and to respond to that person's thoughts and feelings with an appropriate emotion' (Baron-Cohen, 2011, p. 11).

Empathy has both cognitive and affective aspects (Blake and Gannon, 2008). To 'empathise' comprises of both recognising the thoughts and feelings of others and then responding in an appropriate way. For example, if your best friend tells you she has just found out that she has an incurable illness and only has weeks to live, an 'empathic response' would be to recognise and feel the pain, fear and sense of injustice she is likely to be experiencing, and to respond by offering your love and support, not suggesting she should not bother to make any long-term investments or travel plans! Empathy is only possible if you have Theory of Mind (ToM).

Do you regard it as stating the obvious that altruism is rooted in empathy? Probably you do. In case you do not, be assured that most (but not all) of the scholarly work on the topic suggests that it is so. For a long while clinical psychologists, in trying to explain crime, have postulated that those who offend and/or engage in anti-social behaviour have less empathy than those who do not (Hogan, 1969; D. Burke, 2001). Empathy encourages altruistic and pro-social behaviour by helping to identify and share the thoughts and feelings of others, thus working to inhibit their own behaviour. As such, empathy is seen as an important individual protective factor (Jolliffe and Farrington, 2004), exemplified by the fact that 'empathy enhancement' is a central plank in many programmes aimed at reducing individual offending (R. Ross and Ross, 1995). Psychopaths have long been considered those most likely to be violent (and to re-offend), with low empathy a central component.

Empathy thus arguably lies at the root of 'pro-social behaviour' (Zahn-Waxler and Robinson, 1995) and its absence at the root of crime (when the law is regarded as fair). If you can empathise with people, you are more likely to avoid hurting them. Empathy represents an obstacle to causing people distress (Feshbach, 1987; P. A. Miller and Eisenberg, 1988). Results of the systematic review by Darrick Jolliffe and David Farrington suggest that there is a consensus in the literature that empathy and crime are linked and that you can measure empathy (2004, p. 442). You can think of it either as a continuous variable (e.g. low to high empathy), or as a risk factor (e.g. lack of empathy versus presence of empathy) (2004, p. 442). They conclude from their own review that offending and empathy are negatively related (less empathy, more crime) but this relationship appears to be influenced by a number of factors, so it's complicated. Cognitive empathy has a stronger negative relationship with offending than has affective empathy (Jolliffe and Farrington, 2004).

In brief, empathy research with regard to crime and other anti-social behaviours suggests that those good at empathising are less likely to commit it (P. A. Miller and Eisenberg, 1988; Zahn-Waxler and Robinson, 1995), making empathy a player in any explanation why most of us tend (*most of the time and in ways that we think really matter*) to stick to the rules and obey 'the law'. There is much yet to explain, and the interested reader should keep her eye out for new research on the link. Jolliffe and Farrington (2004) suggest that what are needed to clarify the relationship between low empathy and offending are better measures of empathy (i.e. more robust tools) and self-reports in prospective longitudinal studies.

In an effort to produce a more robust measurement tool, Simon Baron-Cohen and colleagues have developed the 'Empathy Quotient' (a questionnaire based tool designed to measure levels of empathy in the general population) which has found that 'broad bands' of empathy exist within which, from day to day, we might move around a little as a result of 'transient fluctuations', but which are essentially 'broadly fixed' (Baron-Cohen, 2011, p. 16). Bands range from 'Level 0' where individuals have absolutely no empathy (e.g. psychopaths, see Box 3.2), through to 'Level Six' where individuals are total empaths, having 'remarkable empathy, [and] who are continuously focused on other people's feelings and go out of their way to check on these and be supportive'(Baron-Cohen, 2011, p. 18).

The fluctuations in empathy within an individual are important, because they identify the scope for manipulating environments. From a crime prevention perspective, the task is to identify those environments, settings and situations which might reduce, and those which might increase, individual levels of empathy and so increase or reduce the chances of criminal behaviour – empathy playing a role of 'individual protective factor' (Jolliffe and Farrington, 2004). This is merely introduced here but is expanded upon in Chapter 7.

David Farrington suggests that offenders are 'callous with low empathy' (Farrington, 1998, p. 257), which probably explains why most of the recent empathy research with offenders has concentrated on those who commit violent and/or sexual offences (L. E. Marshall and Marshall, 2011).

L. E. Marshall and Marshall (2011), in discussion of a model of empathy proposed by W. L. Marshall *et al.* (1995), claim that a number of 'predictions can

---

Box 3.2   How to spot a psychopath

We are not sure of the provenance of the following scenario although rumour has it that it originates with the United States FBI. It is more probable, however, that it is an example of 'folk-law' in action. Either way, we use it to illustrate how those deemed 'psychopaths' are commonly perceived to think and behave.

A woman attends the funeral of her beloved sister. At what is understandably a very emotional occasion for her and her family, she notices a rather handsome male stranger. She does not get the opportunity to speak to him during the service, but nor does she get a chance afterwards as he does not show up at the wake. A few days later she kills her mother. Why?

The 'psychopathic' answer to this question is quite simple. The woman killed her mother in order to trigger another family funeral; one likely to be attended by the same attendees, including, most importantly, the mysterious male stranger. In this scenario, the murder of the mother by her daughter is regarded as 'instrumental' in orchestrating a second opportunity to meet the possible 'man of her dreams' and an example of 'psychopathic thinking'.

We offer a few words of comfort for readers who correctly answer the question above. Fear not, we do not at this juncture consider that getting the question correct is sufficient reason for you to worry about being a psychopath. Take a look at the work of Robert Hare, and you will soon see that diagnosing psychopathy is a far more complex and detailed assessment process.

We pose the question of whether having a psychopathic personality, of which a lack of empathy is a key element, is a kind of 'evolutionary throwback' to before we became the social species we are today. What do you think?

---

be made about where empathy deficits originate' (2011, p. 744). This is reproduced (in part) below:

1   Insofar as an individual is oblivious to the emotions of others there is no reason for the empathic process to begin.
2   If the individual lacks perspective-taking or ToM they might not understand why the individual is distressed, and so the empathic process would be impaired.
3   If the individual recognises the distress of another but is indifferent to or enjoys it, he or she would not feel impelled to alleviate it.
4   If the individual recognises the stress of another but is too overwhelmed by the need to 'self-soothe' (i.e. too concerned about their own feelings) they will not be able to complete the empathic process.

Although admittedly Marshall's model of empathy (W. L. Marshall *et al.*, 1995) has been consistent with research with sex offenders (Hudson *et al.*, 1993; Gery *et al.*, 2009), this group has been found less accurate at recognising the emotions of others and in perspective-taking than control groups. Recognition of the fact that there is a link between the absence of empathic awareness and *feeling* and criminal *action* has spawned the plethora of empathy-inducing offender rehabilitation programmes now available. These generally focus on improving the empathy levels of offenders, particularly by encouraging individuals to acknowledge and understand the hurt (including emotional distress) which they cause the victims of their crimes, an approach especially favoured in sex offender change programmes (L. E. Marshall and Marshall, 2011). This is ironic, given that the systematic review mentioned earlier showed that the relationship between lack of empathy and crime was *weakest* for sex offenders (Jolliffe and Farrington, 2004). So much for empathy deficit amongst offenders and what to do about it.

Empathy in religion and law

There is an ever-present danger in criminology of seeing the offender as the proper focus of attention. How about religious and criminal justice practitioners and citizens watching the crime and justice drama being played out before them? They are the products of evolution just as much as the offender. We touch on this topic briefly only to make the point that responses to crime are as much a subject for scholarship as the crime itself.

The great religions invoke empathy, or its synonym compassion:

'They ask thee how much they are to spend (in charity); say: "What is beyond your needs".'

(Qur'ān 2:219)

'Teacher, which is the greatest commandment in the Law?' Jesus replied: 'Love the Lord your God with all your heart and with all your soul and with all your mind.' This is the first and greatest commandment. And the second is like it: 'Love your neighbour as yourself.' All the Law and the Prophets hang on these two commandments.

(Matthew 22: 36–40)

Early legal codes such as the Babylonian Code of Hammurabi[5] of 1772 BC reads as remarkably modern, in its insistence on fair dealing between citizens. For example, its Article 9 specifies procedures surrounding evidence necessary to establish whether goods have been stolen.

If a man has lost property and some of it be detected in the possession of another, and the holder has said, 'A man sold it to me, I bought it in the presence of witnesses'; and if the claimant has said, 'I can bring witnesses who know it to be property lost by me'; then the alleged buyer on his part shall produce the man who sold it to him and the witnesses before whom he bought it; the claimant shall on his part produce the witnesses who know it to be his lost property. The judge shall examine their pleas. The witnesses to the sale and the witnesses who identify the lost property shall state on oath what they know. Such a seller is the thief and shall be put to death. The owner of the lost property shall recover his lost property. The buyer shall recoup himself from the seller's estate.

The criminal justice system is shot through with behaviour motivated by empathy *or its lack*. Are there empathy differences between the general community on the one hand, and police officers, prison guards and judges on the other? If so, is it a product of recruitment on the basis of pre-existing personality differences, or does experience in the job create or increase any differences? Do empathic judges impose harsher or more lenient sentences, depending on whether it is the offender or the victim with whom more empathy is felt? We know the answer to none of these interesting questions. As a general rule in social science, it is the powerless rather than the powerful who tend to be the objects of study. We study prisoners not judges, children and the aged not adults, and so on. But standing back from the particular questions about how actors in the criminal justice system behave, consider why the system as a whole exists. It exists to ensure that within-group competition is regulated so that group trust and cooperation survive, as the evolution of our species ordained.

As we noted in the last chapter (and will again in the next), the most remarkable testament to collective altruism (allied to collective self-interest) is the existence of the criminal law itself. It is important not to romanticise criminal justice, but done properly it reflects empathy for crime victims and those who might become crime victims and those who offend insofar as it seeks to ensure humane treatment and rehabilitation. At its (rare) best, it seeks to ensure that citizens who want to live a quiet, cooperative life can do so (to paraphrase Article 8 of the European Convention on Human Rights). As was stressed earlier, there is never a perfect fit between behaviour proscribed by the law and behaviour which meets with widespread disapproval. But we are trespassing into a discussion of the third thing you need to be a pro-social person, which we postpone to the next chapter.

The empathy circuit

Can brain imaging progress our search for empathy? Scientists using Functional Magnetic Resonance Imaging (fMRI) have provisionally identified at least ten interconnected brain regions involved in making up what Simon Baron-Cohen refers to as the 'empathy circuit' (Baron-Cohen, 2011, p. 19).[6]

The existence of the empathy circuit marks out the concept of empathy as something more substantial than a mere psychological construct. De Waal (2009) sees it as a very old pre-human structure. It comprises those areas of the brain identified as being important for social interaction such as perspective-taking and identifying other people's thoughts and feelings. Such areas include the Medial Prefrontal Cortex (Amodio and Frith, 2006). The Medial Prefrontal Cortex overlaps with the Orbito-frontal Cortex which is believed to affect social judgement and the Frontal Operculum which is not only part of the empathy circuit but also involved with language expression (Baron-Cohen, 2011). We also mention the Caudal Anterior Cingulate Cortex (also known as the Middle Cingulate Cortex) because neuroscientists have found that this area of the brain is activated when you see someone in pain whom you like and judge to be fair. Interestingly, Singer and colleagues found that when they saw someone in pain whom they neither liked nor regarded as being fair, on average men showed less activity in this area than women (Singer *et al.*, 2006). We will re-visit the implications of this a little later in the chapter.

The *Mirror Neuron System* has been identified in humans and other animals (see Box 3.3 for a wider discussion of whether animals can empathise). This is perhaps the most exciting neuroscience development informing empathy. The initial work was done on macaque monkeys, and it is the monkey research which will be described in Box 3.3. But there is supporting research on people, using brain imaging and with people who require brain surgery; this makes it possible to carry out investigations into mirror neurons at the same time.

Box 3.3   Can other animals empathise?

Primatologist Frans de Waal argues that other species are capable of empathy because evolutionary theory predicts cognitive similarities based on relations between species and their habitats (de Waal, 2009). This means that if species are closely related (such as wallabies and kangaroos, dolphins and porpoises or chimpanzees and humans) they show similar responses in similar circumstances. De Waal suggests that the 'most parsimonious interpretation' is therefore that cognition involved is similar too. In his view the precursors of empathy are visible in a number of animal behaviours.

In *Putting the altruism back into altruism: the evolution of empathy* (2008) de Waal presents numerous examples of how other mammals display aspects of empathy such as 'emotional contagion' and 'concern'. For example, female vervet monkeys often run to support their young if their play-fighting gets too rough and their infant screams. Bonobos embrace and kiss their opponents after a fight, seemingly in an act of reconciliation and to restore social harmony to the group. 'Mirror neurons' have been found in macaques which are thought to facilitate human imitation and empathy. These fire both when an individual macaque performs an action and when they see or hear another perform that action (de Waal, 2009).

But are these examples of empathy or can they be explained in other ways? Baron-Cohen (2011) is a little more sceptical perhaps: 'Whatever glimmerings of empathy we can discern (or imagine we discern) in other species, the level of empathy that humans show is qualitatively different to that seen in any other species' (2011, p. 98). What do you think?

The most recent generally accessible account of the mirror and canonical neuron story at the time of writing is provided by Marco Iacoboni (Iacoboni, 2009). What he thinks these cells are about is clear from the subtitle of his book *The science of empathy and how we connect with others*. These cells are amazing, almost impossible. One of the (several) accounts of their discovery goes as follows. Vittorio Gallese, a Parma neurophysiologist, was between activities, but his macaque subject was sitting quietly by. Gallese reached for something and there was a burst of activity from a cell in the macaque's brain. Other observations of cells in the same brain area firing when the experimenter did something followed. Cells in the brain that send signals to other cells that are connected to muscles have no business firing when the person or animal is completely still. But they do. These are mirror neurons. It gets weirder. The same mirror neurons are activated when you carry out an action and when you see someone else doing it. Another neuron type, the canonical neuron, is activated when you merely see an object that can be manipulated in a particular way. It is as though your brain were forseeing a possible interaction with that object and preparing for it. It is surely not fanciful to see canonical neurons as the cellular substrate for all kinds of behaviour which may have had survival value. In its relevance for empathy, it seems to anticipate the kinds of action which will be necessary to mesh socially with others. A strange postscript (and an addition to the list of 'things that shouldn't happen') is work on two-year-old children who, if we were right earlier, have not yet developed a sense of empathy. Despite that,

> 2-year-old children's sympathetic arousal, as measured by relative changes in pupil dilation, is similar when they themselves help a person and when they see that person being helped by a third party (and sympathetic arousal in both cases is different from that when the person is not being helped at all). These results demonstrate that the intrinsic motivation for young children's helping behavior does not require that they perform the behavior themselves and thus 'get credit' for it, but rather requires only that the other person be helped.
> (Hepach *et al.*, 2012, p. 967)

This point is developed in the discussion of affordance later in the book.

Simon Baron-Cohen feels that some scholars may have been too quick to assume that mirror neurons equate with empathy and that instead they are more like the 'building blocks' for it (Baron-Cohen, 2011). He offers by way of example the fact that we almost always yawn when we see someone else yawning. This he states is more akin to 'mimicry', the mirroring of the actions of someone else without consciously thinking about their emotional state. Psychologists call this 'the chameleon effect', often an unconscious and shallow behavioural response wholly different to empathy, which is considered emotionally deeper and more complex than a simple, often automatic response. We will see.

We end our brief exploration of some of the brain areas so far identified by scientists to be implicated in the neurobiology of empathy with the *amygdala*. The amygdala is situated in the centre of the *limbic system*, described as 'the emotional brain' because it is involved with how we come to fear things (LeDoux, 1998).

Recognising our own fear and fear in others is an important aspect of being able to empathise. But what's so good about being able to empathise?

We humans have evolved the ability to be empaths: to share feelings, thoughts and emotions, and to show empathic concern not just for other humans but for other sentient creatures too. We can also imagine what other people's lives and situations must be like – we can 'feel for them', even if we have never even met them. Empathy can be plausibly considered as 'a chief enabling process for altruism' (Batson, 2009, p. 3).

Decety argues that there is an 'evolutionary continuity' in the neurobiological systems which provide the basis for empathy and caring. Moreover, 'the relations between emotion, empathic concern, and pro-social behaviour operate on a series of nested evolutionary processes, which are intertwined with social, motivational contingencies, and also subject to contextual control' (2011, p. 41).

Put simply, these things hang together, folks. Evidence from research focused specifically on the neurobiology involved in making charitable donations suggests that acting empathically does not only get us positive social feedback from others (newspapers love to print stories about empathy driven altruistic acts such as running round the world for charity or rescuing cats from trees) but that we are also rewarded 'biologically'. It appears we get to feel good about being empathic and caring partly because the neurotransmitter *dopamine* is released through the projection of neural pathways from the brainstem to the 'nucleus accumbens' (Moll *et al.*, 2006). Of course this is a perfect illustration of how altruism may have developed. Getting a dopamine rush from altruism rewarded further altruistic acts. Those altruistic acts led other group members to favour the altruist. This led to cooperation and sharing which over generations increased the proportion of those experiencing strong dopamine rushes.

Most of the different components of Baron-Cohen's 'empathy circuit' are found in the frontal lobes of the brain. This is the 'newest' part of the brain in evolutionary terms. A search for a reason for the evolution of empathy (our 'new kid' on the cognition block) brings us back to our hypothesis that advanced levels of human social cognition have arisen because of adaptive pressures operating on our relatively recent ancestors.

As we have already highlighted, an evolutionary criminological approach must be about providing explanations for the *whys* of crime and criminality by recourse to 'ultimate causes and motivations' and *how* (e.g. which types of crime are likely?), *where* (i.e. in what contexts and situations are they most likely?) and *when* (i.e. in what circumstances and at what times?) these are most likely to influence or promote criminal and anti-social behaviour in the 'here and now'. To say that crime is simply the product of behaviours that were once adaptive and that are now maladaptive (i.e. illegal and can land you in prison) is not enough.

The story so far and reprise

Previous chapters have illustrated the overwhelming evidence for the theory of evolution, and the mechanism (including kin selection and the reputation economy) whereby pro-social behaviour could confer a selection advantage to altruists. This chapter has identified three necessary conditions underpinning altruism: a theory of mind (ToM), empathy and a sense of fairness. The first two of these were discussed in this chapter, and also the neuroscience evidence for an empathy circuit in the brain. Mirror and canonical neurons were described, and their implications touched upon. The next chapter will deal with the third necessary condition for pro-social behaviour, a sense of fairness.

4 The sense of fairness and the emergence of criminal justice

Introduction

We hope the last chapter clarified the role of Theory of Mind (ToM) and empathy in inclining people towards, or away from, pro-social behaviour. We need a *theory of mind* to have empathy. We need *empathy* to discern unfairness in ways which correspond to those which the direct victims of unfairness suffer. The third element which we took to be necessary for pro-social behaviour was a sense of fairness. The sense of fairness added to empathy is necessary to decide what to do to establish a system of remedies so that cooperative social functioning crucial to our ancestors' survival is maintained. In other words, empathy without some idea what to do with it is useless. The structure of televised charity appeals has three common strands:

1   The people or animals we are trying to help have thoughts and feelings like you;
2   Feel their pain;
3   It's not fair, and this is where you must send your money to make it right.

How readily do people acquire a sense of fairness? The answer is – remarkably readily. As several times before, we appeal to the reader's experience, as a product of evolution like us. One of us is a vegetarian. A few times, when meat in the fridge is about to cease to be edible and others in the family decline to eat it, he has been known to eat it himself. His justification (a technique of neutralisation as criminologists have termed it) is that it's bad enough killing the animal in the first place, but then failing to eat its meat is adding insult to injury. This justification does not save him. When anything goes wrong in the days following his lapse into carnivory (if there is such a word) he attributes it to his wickedness in eating the meat. He knows it is ridiculous, and he hates himself for it, but that is what he thinks. Rabbi Harold Kushner recounts the story of his visit to the home of a young woman who had died suddenly. The first words of the parents were 'You know, Rabbi, we didn't fast last Yom Kippur' (Kushner, 1981, p. 8). Many sufferers from obsessive–compulsive disorder (OCD) explain their compulsions as necessary actions to avoid bad consequences.

We are talking here about immanent justice, where badness automatically brings about retribution. The Swiss psychologist Jean Piaget told children stories (Piaget, 1932). For example a child steals, and later the bridge over which he is walking collapses. Many children interpret the bridge collapse as a consequence of the theft. Much research has been undertaken on how the child processes information to arrive at the idea of Nature or God taking revenge for misdeeds (Karniol, 1980). As Numbers 32:23 in the Bible threatens 'be sure your sin will find you out'.

Perhaps the most interesting is the contention that immanent justice thinking is *more* prevalent in adults than it is in children (Raman and Winer, 2004). One study with adults showed that they exhibited more immanent justice thinking when the maxim 'What goes around comes around' was included in the stories they were told. As one person reflected,

> I know that bad things happen to both good and bad people, but I believe that there is a greater chance of bad things happening to bad people. This person [in the story] was not a good person. He had cheated and lied, and he has robbed many decent people of their money. I know that illnesses like this happen to both good and bad people, but I believe serious illnesses happen at least slightly more to people who deserve them.
>
> (Raman and Winer, 2002, p. 346)

Immanent justice has been linked with the 'just world' hypothesis (Lerner, 1980), which posits that people need to believe in a world where people generally get what they deserve, which allows them to believe they inhabit a stable and orderly niche. Perhaps this is behind the notion of karmic debt, whereby suffering is a consequence of evil deeds in a previous life. By believing in karmic debt, you can believe in immanent justice, 'inexorable and relentless' in spite of the evidence before you. One can rephrase this as saying that it allows people to inhabit a world where trust, and the reputation economy, can prevail over selfishness.

> If the virtuous man who has not done any evil act in this birth suffers, this is due to some wrong act that he may have committed in his previous birth. He will have his compensation in his next birth. If the wicked man who daily does many evil actions apparently enjoys [happiness] in this birth, this is due to some good Karma he must have done in his previous birth. He will have compensation in his next birth. He will suffer in the next birth. The law of compensation is inexorable and relentless.
>
> (Swami Shivananda, *Practice of Karma Yoga*,
> Divine Life Society, 1985, p. 102)

For scholars of the Bible, the notion of the scapegoat echoes the notion of immanent justice. Punishment for sin being inevitable (immanent justice) the burden of the sin is placed on some poor innocent goat, which is then driven into the desert.

'But the goat, on which the lot fell to be the scapegoat, shall be presented alive before the Lord, to make an atonement with him, *and* to let him go for a scapegoat into the wilderness' (Leviticus 16:10).

It was a common practice to tie a red strip of cloth to the scapegoat. The red strip represented the sin of the people which was atoned for. According to the Jewish Talmud this red strip would eventually turn white, signalling God's acceptance of the offering.[1]

Poor bloody goat.

In Christian theology, Jesus Christ was the ultimate scapegoat.

Appealing again to your own experience, what does your gut say when you read about unpleasant people winning the lottery? Do you rejoice in their good fortune, or conclude that something is wrong, that God is asleep at the switch? The tone of police frustration and malice has been evident in all press reports of such cases that we have ever encountered, such as the one in Box 4.1.

In brief, immanent justice judgements help sustain belief in a just world, which is why the reward of the undeserving and the suffering of the worthy are so troubling to us. What has all this got to do with evolution? We earlier accepted the argument that natural selection favoured groups which cooperate internally, but that within groups it favoured selfish individuals, and that this created a tension. The idea that vice will be punished *automatically*, insofar as it is believed, provides an extremely useful constraint on selfish behaviour. The important insight that immanent justice thinking *increases* with age, albeit in more sophisticated forms, suggests that, even now, we are primed to think in that way, with OCD sufferers representing the unfortunate downside of the generally pro-social belief. We introduced the notion of a meme earlier, an idea or theme (as replicator) which uses people as survival vehicles. The grandmother of one of us, dead for some fifty-five years, successfully planted the meme 'Be sure your sins will find you out' in the conscience of the still guilt-ridden second author![2]

Are we really primed to think in terms of fairness? Mark Pagel thinks we are. He writes: 'Of all the emotions associated with getting acts of reciprocity to work, our expectation for fairness is perhaps the most intriguing and explosive' (Pagel, 2012, p. 195). He cites the results of 'the ultimatum game' in support of his position. The game runs as follows. Person 1 is given a sum of money (say £100) and told he has to give some of it to Person 2 (whom he is told he will never get to meet). Person 2 knows how much money Person 1 has to give and can accept or reject the offer. If the offer is rejected, *neither person gets anything*. The rational thing for Person 1 to do is to offer a very small amount. The rational thing for Person 2 to do is to accept whatever is offered (since something is better than nothing). Pagel reports that the game has been played with many groups in cultures around the world, and that people generally do not behave in this rational way. Person 1's typical offer is 40 per cent of the total available. Person 2 rejects offers substantially below this proportion as 'unfair', though loses out by doing so. Pagel accounts for the irrational behaviour as follows:

> You can be told the exchange is anonymous and that you will never encounter the person again, but that does not mean you can simply switch off the normal emotions that natural selection has created in us. . . . The experimenters who

Box 4.1   Sick thug ripped off taxpayers in £13,000 benefits scam after £5m jackpot win

Sick lotto rapist Edward Putman flashed an arrogant grin as he left court after admitting a £13,000 benefits scam.

The 46-year-old now faces jail for lying about a £5 million win so he could carry on ripping off taxpayers while splashing out his fortune on fancy sports cars and a £600,000 home.

But that clearly did not seem to bother the jobless thug, who spent seven years in jail for a violent sex attack on a teenage girl more than 20 years ago.

Putman tried to hide his face under a hood and with sun specs after he admitted two counts of benefit fraud.

His payments were stopped in December 2009 after he failed to show up for a medical assessment, three months after he scooped £4.9 million on the lottery.

At the time of the win he asked for no publicity.

Prosecutor Hita Mashru told the court: 'You may see that it's very clear why. He has previous convictions and the fact that he was claiming benefits.

'Records show that in the days after winning the lottery he bought sports cars and a house. It's very calculating.'

Putman, of Kings Langley, Herts, was caught when he tried to buy his council flat for £83,000 in cash.

He had even kept his windfall from his family, St Albans magistrates heard.

Ten months later he sent a letter to the DSS begging for his benefits to be reinstated.

The conman wrote: 'I've not supported myself very well, my rent hasn't been paid, and I'm on the border of being evicted, no bills have been paid, I don't eat as my stomach will not hold it down.

'Money I have managed to get has been from selling my belongings, as I will not need them, as I expect to be evicted.'

Putman, who threatened to kill the teen he raped in Milton Keynes, Bucks, will be sentenced at St Albans crown court on July 24.

Lotto rapist number one was Iorworth Hoare, 59, of Newcastle, who won £7 million in 2004 after buying a ticket on day release from jail.

http://www.mirror.co.uk/news/uk-news/edward-putman-lottery-rapist-admits-1131857 (accessed 25 September 2012).

conduct these studies are, in effect, asking their volunteers to leave behind at the door all of the evolved psychology for long-term relations.

(p. 199)

Enter, criminal law

Sometimes the fear of immanent justice is not enough to deter people from exploitative behaviour, and groups decide collectively (or by leader dictat) to set up arrangements whereby the group as a whole sanctions those who exploit others in the group. Every sports or social club has rules whose breach leads to sanction (usually fines or expulsion). At the national or regional level, there exists criminal law. The difference between civil law and criminal law is instructive. Civil law regulates relations between citizens, the state offering its services as adjudicator as to who has wronged whom and how the wrong can be righted. In criminal law, the state and the allegedly erring citizen are the conflicting parties. In effect, the state is saying that the alleged wrongdoing is so serious that society itself rather than the individual victim is the main interested party in the conflict. Some criminologists have argued that virtually all law ought to be civil law, because conflicts are people's property, and the state is in effect stealing their conflicts from them (Christie, 1977). The counter-argument is that the overarching interest is in eliminating threats to cooperation at the group level, rather than person to person vengeance.

It is important to stress that the criminal law is designed for within-nation conflicts. Between-nation conflicts are addressed by other means, probably of different evolutionary origin. First let us state what lawyers say the criminal law is about. The American Law Institute Model Penal Code sets out the purposes succinctly:

- To forbid and prevent conduct that unjustifiably and inexcusably inflicts or threatens substantial harm to individual or public interests;
- To subject to public control persons whose conduct indicates that they are disposed to commit crimes;
- To safeguard conduct that is without fault from condemnation as criminal;
- To give fair warning of the nature of the conduct declared to be an offence;
- To differentiate on reasonable grounds between serious and minor offences.

In short, it sets out to protect citizens from other citizens, by telling them what they can't do, by acting against them when they do what they are not supposed to, by controlling them, by being proportionate in the response to offending and by protecting citizens who have done no wrong from persecution by other citizens. But the Code (and common sense) tempers justice with mercy. The Code sets out to control 'persons whose conduct indicates that they are disposed to commit crimes', not just anyone who misbehaves. An important element in the judgement of most crimes is *mens rea*, a guilty mind (Ormerod, 2011). This is true of adults but not of children. As a child grows, intention comes to the fore in judgements of wrongdoing (Piaget, 1932). This would also have made sense in the Environment of Evolutionary Adaptation (EEA). The group was important. Unintended or atypical behaviour, if sanctioned severely, may deprive a small hunting or foraging group of an important member, just as in soccer ejection of a player from the field of play handicaps a team. There is nothing in the Code which is surprising if one thinks in terms of criminal law as a second line of defence (after the fear of immanent justice) in advancing the cause of within-group solidarity. But how do students of evolutionary psychology think about the criminal law? Mostly they don't. In a 723-page tome on *The psychology and law of criminal justice processes* (Levesque, 2006) the word evolution is used once, and then not in the Darwinian sense. Owen Jones' discussion of the topic (O. Jones, 2005) characterises criminal law as 'a tool for moving human animals to behave in ways they would not otherwise behave if left to their own devices' (p. 953).

The most detailed discussion of law and criminal justice using an evolutionary perspective is that of Michael Bang Petersen and his colleagues (Petersen *et al.*, 2010), and this will be described at some length. It is particularly useful because it reconfigures concepts familiar with lawyers and criminologists in terms of evolutionary psychology.

Petersen's starting point is that the problems of exploitation as a threat to social functioning were acute in the EEA, with 'the average person situated in a world full of individuals poised to impose costs on him or her if such acts were beneficial' (p. 73). This resulted in mental programmes to 'recalibrate certain behaviour-regulating variables in the mind of the perpetrator and other potential exploiters' (p. 72). Whether this takes the form of punishment or reconciliation depends upon a number of circumstances, including whether the exploiter is a relative, the closeness of collaborative links between victim and exploiter, and the risk of counter-measures (whether the exploiter was big and strong and had loyal friends). Petersen and colleagues suggest that people have a set of internal regulatory variables (e.g. how hungry or tired am I?). Such internal regulatory variables sustain welfare-tradeoff ratios (WTRs) which are applied to the specific facts of an exploitative event. WTRs are taken to be ubiquitous. How much effort or inconvenience am I prepared to suffer to advance another's welfare by a given amount? WTRs can be thought of as person specific in two ways, which we can term personality and preference variation. As for personality, at the saintly extreme, someone is prepared to give small benefits to others (any others) at huge personal cost. At the other extreme, we find someone who would kill a person (anyone) for a few pounds. Thinking about preference, an individual may be prepared to do anything for one person, and nothing for someone else. WTRs are thus actor and other specific, and flexible in the light of new knowledge (for example a man might give a woman a seat on a bus upon learning that she is pregnant).

Simplifying somewhat, the inclination to punish or to seek reconciliation with an exploiter depends upon one's WTR in relation to him or her. So people generally inclined to have high WTRs and/or who are personally and positively linked to the exploiter will generally seek reconciliation; otherwise they are likely to seek punishment. However Petersen and colleagues make an important qualification to this by distinguishing between intrinsic and monitored WTRs. Intrinsic WTRs are those which apply when the decision will not be made public, monitored WTRs when they will. This is relevant to jury selection and witness intimidation. The decision to punish the exploiter under monitored conditions decreases if

1   The exploiter is big and strong;
2   The exploiter has big strong friends;
3   The exploiter has high social status and valued skills;
4   The exploiter is rich.

Please don't forget that we are here discussing EEA, not the present day, so what counted as rich then is more in terms of meat than banker bonuses.

Petersen continues 'fitness benefits flow from being with people who care about your welfare and attend to the welfare consequences of their actions' (p. 84). This has implications for group schism in EEA and arguably for the crime-driven decision to move home in modern times, with consequences for the creation of high crime neighbourhoods. Accordingly, across cultures, acts that indicate a low WTR are set apart, and a criminal justice system coalesces around them. There is evidence of cross-cultural consensus in the harm (signals low WTR) which is reflected in their criminalisation and differential sanction levels (Stylianou, 2003). An example of rated seriousness of a range of offences is provided as Box 4.2. You would be unusual if your ranking of seriousness deviated

---

Box 4.2   Hierarchy of crime seriousness (Taken from Pease, 1988)

Murder
Robbery with Violence
Sexual Offence against a child under 13
Cruelty to children
Indecent assault on woman
Causing death by dangerous driving
Manslaughter
Fraud
Housebreaking
Breaking into a factory
Stealing (without violence)
Fighting (common assault)
Taking away a motor vehicle without owner's consent
Being drunk and disorderly
Stealing by finding
Travelling on a bus without paying the fare
Vagrancy

much from that given. It will differ somewhat because of changed values since the work was done in the mid-1980s. Check with your friends too. The agreement is real, extensive and cross-cultural (Pease *et al.*, 1975).

It is possible to manipulate the perceived seriousness of a crime, for example by invoking the exceptional need of the exploiter (I stole to feed my children) or effects on third parties (theft of copper cable from the railway delays thousands of train travellers).

Petersen and colleagues explore in much more detail the cognitive mechanisms of the central decision about how to deal with exploiters and should be read in the original. However it is believed that the description above captures the essence of their view. We now consider how differences between the modern world and the EEA might cause problems for criminal justice arrangements. The first and central difference is that we now need a system, and a very elaborate and expensive system it is too. When group size was limited by the Dunbar number, those with deviant WTRs would be detected by their behaviour across time, known to the group as a whole. The arrangements for sanction or reconciliation would be administered by those who knew the exploiters and their value to the group.

We cannot go back to the EEA. The next best thing is anthropological study of surviving hunter-gatherer bands. Chris Boehm (2012) has trawled the relevant literature to distinguish the kind of sanctions which are mentioned for each of the studied groups in at least one anthropologist's report. The results are shown as Table 4.1. It will be seen that there is the mixture of punishment and reconciliation

Table 4.1 Sanctions for crime

Sanction	n/10
Entire group kills culprit	6
Nominee assassinates culprit	6
Permanent expulsion from group	4
Public opinion	10
Gossip (as private expression of public opinion)	9
Ridicule	10
Direct criticism by group or spokesman	8
Group shaming	6
Other shaming	5
Spatial distancing (move or re-orient camp)	10
Group ostracism	8
Social aloofness (reduced speaking)	7
Tendency to avoid culprit	5
Total shunning (total avoidance)	5
Temporary expulsion from group	3
Nonlethal physical punishment	10
Administration of blows	5

(Boehm, 2012)

tactics that Petersen assumed. It would be useful to go back to the anthropological literature and see whether the factors identified by Petersen as crucial in determining the 'recalibration' route had been noted by anthropologists.

Christopher Boehm's hunter-gatherer database contains ten groups. The cell entries are the number out of ten where at least one anthropological account mentioned the form of sanction shown in the left row.

To return to the key issue, whereas sanctions in the EEA were administered by the relatively small group of people who knew the exploiter/criminal, that is no longer the case. An impersonal apparatus is set up wherein the decision to proceed officially against an exploiter is taken by people who do not know him, his guilt is assessed by a jury comprising people who do not know him, and the sanction is administered by strangers. The judgements of his WTR are no longer informed by people who know the context and circumstances of the exploitation over time. Perhaps paradoxically, the group which relinquishes the exploiter to strangers is more vulnerable to his friends, fellow gang members, and so on. The only role which people who know the exploiter have in the trial by strangers is that of witness, with the endemic problem of witness intimidation in crime challenged areas. Somewhat too simply, consigning an exploiter to the criminal justice system is consigning a member of the in-group to the tender mercies of an out-group. This is what adds power to the accusation that someone is an informer, a 'grass'. This was illustrated the week before writing this. Two unarmed female police officers were murdered, having been lured to a house by a bogus phone call reporting a burglary. The killer had in the previous months killed two other people and tried to kill two more. He was a high risk person, to put it mildly. Yet those who work locally report that he was leading a pretty normal life, despite being sought by the police. The local community did not report him. On the regional news on the night of the police murders, one young man from the area explained 'Nobody likes a grass, do they?' Perhaps the evolved mechanisms of recalibration surface in the recurring attempts of localities to reclaim their right to recalibrate. This is evident in the English rural practice of 'rough music', where pots and pans were hammered outside the homes of miscreants (Thompson, 1972), commented on as follows:[3]

> Rough music belongs to a mode of life in which some part of the law belongs still to the community and is theirs to enforce. It indicates modes of social self-control and the disciplining of certain kinds of violence and anti-social offence . . .

It can also be seen in the parallel criminal justice system operated by paramilitary groups in Northern Ireland (Morrissey and Pease, 1982) and the local justice in South African townships including the use of petrol-filled tyres as burning necklaces to despatch wrongdoers.[4] Finally, it is evident in the wish of many sports officials to treat crimes on the field of play differently from the same actions otherwise processed by criminal law.

A double-edged sword in Petersen's characterisation of EEA justice is its flexibility. In modern criminal justice systems, actions have to be legislated as crimes. In EEA justice, the group simply has to reach a decision that a member's WTR is so out of step that action is necessary. Laws which are out of step with emerging modern sensibilities cause problems.

When Rosa Parks, a black woman, broke the law by refusing to give up her bus seat for a white passenger in Montgomery, Alabama on 1 December 1956, who you felt empathy with depended on your view of the law she was breaking. In the spirit of the place and time, many white people would feel empathy with the white folk whose exclusive rights were being denied by Rosa Parks' action. For those disgusted by discrimination, Rosa Parks was and is fêted as a heroine.[5]

It is as well not to romanticise local justice. Don't forget that women were burned as witches. Not that formal criminal justice would have saved them, as the Salem trials attest. Indeed the last woman to be convicted and branded as a witch was Helen Duncan in 1944, condemned because of her uncanny knowledge of wartime secrets.[6]

Recall the lesson of Chapter 2. Groups with too many free-riders will not do well in competition with other groups. Groups whose local justice means that their members are at each other's throats all the time will not prevail in competition with other groups or in tasks which require cooperation. There is thus a crude self-limiting factor weeding out the most brutal and inept forms of local justice. But groups like this no longer go out of existence. You can find them in crime-riven areas of our cities, consisting predominantly of young males.

Chapter summary and reprise

We have discussed the sense of fairness. We discussed immanent justice, whereby people have a tendency to see punishment as following automatically from misdeeds. We have discussed the mechanism by which our forebears assessed welfare and cost trade-offs of exploitative behaviour before deciding on attempts to punish or reconcile the exploiter. We discussed the mismatch between the current criminal justice system and evolved local, group-based justice.

In the next chapters we will go on to discuss the problems which have conventionally exercised criminologists, to see whether evolutionary thinking can cast new light on old problems.

5 Violence

Many intellectuals have averted their gaze from the evolutionary logic of violence, fearing that acknowledging it is tantamount to accepting or even to approving it.

(Pinker, 2002, p. 336)

Introduction

In this chapter we focus our evolutionary lens on the prevalence, function and likely origins of violent behaviour and on behaviours which forestall or limit the expression of violence. One of the advantages of looking at violence from an evolutionary point of view is that it deals with the violent act directly, not obscured by the forest of exceptions and permissions to be violent provided by criminal law, religion and war. A brief exploration of the origins of violence and its more modern manifestations comprises the substance of this chapter. The separation of this chapter and the one which follows is somewhat arbitrary. In the next chapter we will look at issues of violence, gender and age.

Traditional explanations for violence

One of us has a favourite essay question which he likes to set second year crimi-nology students. It goes as follows 'There are no one-size-fits-all explanations for violence: critically assess this view with reference to two common explanations'. Thoughtful answers typically use two or more explanations to show how violence is too 'slippery' to be explained in all its forms; that is how it is too complex and diverse for any one explanation to handle comprehensively. Think about it: could any one explanation for violence adequately cover diverse violent events such as a suicide bombing at a Turkish market and assaults on elderly residents of care homes and the mass killing of cinema attendees by a lone gunman in the USA?[1]

The acts to which one chooses to attach the tag *violent* are determined by culture and history. The word has overtones of disapproval. The same physical actions can be sanitised by using alternative words or completely excused as acts of war. For example, the smacking of a child has recently been prohibited by English law as constituting violence towards children. The same actions would be called tough love or discipline by its advocates. In soccer games, euphemisms like 'Let him know you're there' really mean 'assault him'. Rioters exhibit violence, the police contain it or 'defuse the situation'. Murderers kill, states retaining the death penalty exact justice. Men violent towards their partner 'give her a smack'. Two-year-olds have 'temper tantrums' in which they strain every muscle to inflict maximum damage on their carer. When insurgents and unlucky civilians are killed in drone attacks, news reports tend to say that 'x people *died* in the attacks', somehow distancing the explosive cause of their death from its result. And let us not get into the bizarre language of martyrdom. In short, by a mixture of political legerdemain and self-interest, the boundaries of violent action are drawn and re-drawn.

Explanations for violence cut across all the social sciences and beyond to biological science and the pub at the end of your street, and are listed and described in most mainstream criminology texts (Athens, 1989; Blackburn, 1993; S. Jones, 2000; Newburn, 2007). Such texts provide a broad enough array of explanations for the reader to appreciate the subjectivity and complexity involved in defining and explaining violence, without listing them here. Common popular explanations include poor parenting, deprivation, watching violent television programmes, playing vile computer games, class conflict, psychopathology, blocked aspirations, poor diet, drugs (including alcohol) and peer pressure (see S. Jones, 2000; R. H. Burke, 2005; or Newburn, 2007 for more comprehensive discussions).

Some of the oft-quoted explanations such as deprivation and poor educational attainment suffer from what Marcus Felson (1994) calls the pestilence fallacy. He notes that crime, including violent crime, has changed more in line with the provision of opportunities than it has with levels of economic deprivation. Also, poverty does not explain domestic abuse by high status males. Let us be clear. We are not cheerleaders for poverty. There are plenty of good reasons other than violence reduction for seeking to reduce poverty. Evolutionary explanations, focusing on a different kind of impoverishment, namely the lack of opportunities for reproductive success, may fare better.

Buss and Shackelford (1997) contend that some human violence is 'ubiquitous', across all times and societies, which means that it cannot be explained solely by the variables of usual criminological interest. For example, criminological or psychological explanations which focus on violence depicted in television programmes and films as an explanation for violent acts on the street will struggle to explain why it was that our ancestors were a more violent bunch than us, despite being denied 'Grand Theft Auto'. The question that evolutionary psychologists ask is: what was in it for the violent person? Did violence enhance reproductive success? If so, how did it do it? Existing criminological explanations for violent behaviour either focus on the present circumstances in which the violence occurred (proximal factors) or on the recent past (distal factors) such as events in the individual's childhood. Only evolutionary explanations for violence go beyond that. If the roots of violence lie in the EEA, this is essential for any approach claiming to be comprehensive. If they do not, evolutionary accounts are indeed just so stories.

What is there to explain? Does every human have the capacity for violence? It certainly does not seem that way. If it were so, surely we would scuttle from place to place, avoiding others and fighting when we met them. But as Chapter 2 showed, we are ultra-social.

Before we go on, this seems to be an appropriate point at which to reiterate a point touched upon earlier, namely that shaped by evolution does not mean uniform across a population. In some cases (for example eye colour) variation exists because natural selection did not confer a selection advantage on one or other variant. In other cases, different genotypes within a species are in a stable or semi-stable equilibrium. To take the most obvious example, a population exclusively of men or exclusively of women would last just one generation. It may be the case that a tribe of the meek would not inherit the earth but would have been slain by a tribe of the violent, but the tribe of the violent would have a hard time of it living peaceably together and, failing to cooperate, would fail to flourish.

Violence: just human nature?

There are in present times happily fewer occasions in which self-defensive or kin-protective violence is necessary. Nonetheless we can all envisage circumstances in which we would kill. The most placid of women can become violent in defence of her children. One of us came off worst once when he tried to intervene in a violent dispute between two mums at a park, over which child's turn it was next on a swing.

In pre-Christian Scandinavia, the berserkers were the elite warriors who 'went berserk', going into battle without armour and acting 'like mad dogs or wolves. They bit into their shields and were as strong as bears or bulls. They killed men, but neither fire nor iron harmed them. This madness is called berserker-fury.'[2] Are you a potential berserker? Stephen Pinker thinks you might be.

Stephen Pinker characterises violence as part of the human design: 'Animals deploy aggression in highly selective ways, and humans, whose limbic systems are enmeshed with outsize frontal lobes, are of course even more calculating. Most people today live their adult lives without ever pressing their violence buttons' (Pinker, 2002, p. 316).

At several points in this book we have asked you to introspect to help judge whether evolved inclinations are in *your* brain. Please now ask yourself, have you ever fantasised about killing someone you personally dislike or hate? University students are not an especially homicidal bunch, but 70–90 per cent of male students asked this kind of question replied that they had. Rather fewer women (but still a clear majority) had also fantasised in this way (Kenrick and Sheets, 1993; Buss, 2005). These were not just vague and generalised thoughts. They often extended to discussions about how the victim would be lured to the place of execution, and precisely how the killing would be carried out. What's more, the envisaged methods were plausible and well thought through. The inference is that most of us have at least the capacity for violence. This is unsurprising in that preparation for and competence in violent acts was a necessary capacity in EEA.

So most (perhaps all) of us contemplate murdering someone, and contemplate it in some detail. Is it most of us or all of us? Stephen Pinker recounts telling a class of students about the Buss research, which found that a majority of students had murderous thoughts. One of his students interjected 'Yes, and the rest are liars' (Pinker, 2011). And those who have actually murdered usually seem very normal, and do have among the lowest rates of reconviction of any offender grouping. One of us has a poignant memory of meeting a convicted murderer for the first time: not his piercing stare or cold, emotionless personality, but how normal he seemed. The second author has worked in a maximum security hospital, and despite the fact that the murderers there had been given a psychiatric diagnostic label, if you had met them in the supermarket, you would happily pass the time of day with them. Those who interview serial killers have often talked about the normality of their subjects (e.g. Morrison and Goldberg, 2004). Friends, neighbours and the wife of Mohammad Sidique Khan, leader of the London 7 July bombers, all said in interviews how 'normal' he was. To summarise, ask normal people whether they have contemplated murder and they come across as potential murderers. Talk to murderers and they generally come across as normal people. And it is a fact that murderers have among the lowest rates of reconviction, far lower than the reconviction rate of short-term prisoners.

In short, what seems universal is the *mental capacity and readiness to consider* lethal violence. As Richard Wortley concludes, 'There can be little doubt that the potential for violence is part of human nature' (2011, p. 30).

The proverb says that the thought is father to the deed. So what determines the transition from common thought to the uncommon action?

Although our violent 'inner demon' survives, its appearance is rare and is contingent on the situation or environment. (Perhaps that is why we find Superman and the Incredible Hulk so appealing. They are peaceable until the situation demands otherwise. The Hulk is you. The Hulk is me.)

Individual differences in recourse to violence

Perhaps the important questions to be addressed are:

1   Do people vary in the environmental threshold which turns them to violence?
2   What are the common environmental triggers to violence that we can manipulate?
3   What are the possible evolutionary origins of violence?

The short answer is that yes, there are such differences. Those diagnosed as psychopaths tend to have short fuses. Interestingly, they show more indignation (i.e. the situations they find provoking are more trivial) than people used for comparison purposes do (Book and Quinsey, 2004). This suggests that the difference lies as much in the interpretation of the situation appropriate for violence as in the disposition. Some personality scales seek to measure such differences (Huesmann *et al.*, 1978; Caprara *et al.*, 1985). There is an emerging technical literature on the evolution of individual differences including aggression (Caprara *et al.*, 1996; Buss and Hawley, 2011). Describing this literature would require a book in itself. We will, however, describe one strand of research of this kind. It is particularly interesting because it completely demolishes the kind of criticism which charges evolutionary perspectives with being insensitive to environmental and cultural influences.

Terrie Moffitt leads a team at King's College London which has done some of the most exciting work of the last century on criminality. In 2002 an article by this group, lead author Avshalom Caspi, made a discovery that was game-changing for the understanding of aggression (Caspi *et al.*, 2002; Kim-Cohen *et al.*, 2006). The 2002 abstract states soberly:

> A functional polymorphism in the gene encoding the neurotransmitter-metabolizing enzyme monoamine oxidase A (*MAOA*) was found to moderate the effect of maltreatment. Maltreated children with a genotype conferring high levels of *MAOA* expression were less likely to develop antisocial problems. These findings may partly explain why not all victims of maltreatment grow up to victimize others, and they provide epidemiological evidence that genotypes can moderate children's sensitivity to environmental insults.
>
> (p. 851)

We have avoided discussion of genetics and the quotation may seem like gobbledegook to you. To clarify for such readers, the Caspi paper shows that a particular genetic variant makes children suffering maltreatment grow up showing a disposition to violence. So the gene effect kicks in only when the child is treated badly. All maltreatment of children should be stopped. The new evidence shows that there are some children on whom maltreatment has a particularly malign effect. If such children are maltreated, we are raising violent people, through no fault of their own, and condemning them, as well as their victims, to much misery.

The next bit is speculative, but provides a tentative evolutionary hypothesis. In communities characterised by much intra-group violence, parents are more likely to be abusive towards their children. A child growing up peaceable would be at a disadvantage, would be bullied and not receive a fair share of resources. It would make sense therefore for a gene variant which sensitises to violence to survive. A child primed for violence by an abusive upbringing is more likely to grow up violent. If such a child grows up in a more peaceable environment with non-abusive parents, he or she is not at much of a disadvantage since the violent tendencies for which they are genetically primed have not been activated by maltreatment. It would be nice to know the prevalence of the sensitising variant in surviving hunter-gatherer groups. The hypothesis would be that it would be found in more people in the more generally violent groupings.

Later work has confirmed the Caspi analysis (Foley *et al.*, 2004) and added complexity in suggesting an interacting effect of ethnicity. Many articles on the topic have been written in the few years since the original Caspi work, and other interactions of a similar kind have emerged. This work hammers home the complexity of the determination of aggressive predispositions in ways which invite evolutionary accounts (Carver *et al.*, 2011).

Environmental triggers

So people vary in their readiness to resort to violence, and get that way as a result of complex gene–environment interactions which invite (but have not yet received) thorough analysis in evolutionary terms. Proclivity to violence will no doubt determine where people spend their time. Elton John had a hit song with 'Saturday night's alright for fighting' whose success must have been in part due to the juxtaposition of the fighting image with the notably unfrightening Elton. Likewise people with prison-made ACAB (all coppers are bastards) tattoos on their knuckles may look out of place in a concert of Schubert songs. Both stereotypes can be knocked down, but by and large, 'birds of a feather flock together'. People to some extent select the environments in which they grow up. Gene-environment dynamics are spectacularly complex.

What is there to say about direct environmental triggers for violence? Difference, authority and frustration are the obvious ones. It is disturbingly easy to create hostile feelings just by creating arbitrary differences between people (Tajfel, 1981). One of the best known was the Stanford Prison Experiment, where random allocation to the role of prisoner and guard was enough to generate hostility (Zimbardo, 2007). Earlier classic studies on conformity all tell the same story. Create a difference and hatred will result. Live in Glasgow or Belfast and your religion and football team determine whom you regard with suspicion and possible hostility. And that is perhaps the interesting thing on which evolution throws light. The groups you hate most are those with whom you might conceivably interact. One of us had a relative (by marriage, now thankfully dissolved) who was a Glasgow Protestant. His daughter was enjoined never to bring a Catholic boy home. If she did, her father threatened, she was no longer his daughter. Presumably she could have brought a Malaysian Satanist home with no problem, but a local Catholic, never! Gangs hate gangs on adjacent turf, Sunnis Shi'ites, Orthodox Jews Reform Jews, and so on. During the EEA, it was your neighbouring groups with which you were in competition. There was no point being prepared for conflict with distant groups, because you didn't know distant groups existed. It was those who might hunt and forage on your turf who were the problem.

The second central variable determining hostility triggers is authority. The obedience studies of Stanley Milgram are too well known to need describing in detail here (Milgram, 1974). In essence they showed that people were prepared to conform with the dictates of authority even when they thought it was leading them to administer potentially lethal electric shocks. Much about this is to be found in the Zimbardo book mentioned just now. Put too simply, he moves the cause of violence from person to situation to system, system being situation plus authority. The hunter-gatherer groups that Boehm studied all seem to have had authority arrangements necessary for cooperative food acquisition (Boehm, 2012). Christopher Browning's 1992 book *Ordinary men* tells the chilling story of how a unit of ordinary, middle-aged German reserve policemen in 1942, *under orders*, liquidated a Jewish village as part of the Nazis' 'final solution'. More recent genocide in the former Yugoslavia and Rwanda, sometimes referred to as 'ethnic cleansing' by those seeking justification for their abhorrent acts of cruelty, stand as more contemporary examples of how situations and contexts can release the inner demon.

The third thing which moves people towards violence is frustration. The particular aspect of frustration stemming from sexual rivalry will be discussed in the next chapter, but the classic psychological theory of violence is the 'frustration–aggression' hypothesis, which holds that aggression is the response to the expected interference with a desired goal (Dollard *et al.*, 1939; see also Berkowitz's 1989 reformulation). Perhaps the classic demonstration of the link comes from research showing that in the southern USA, there was an association between the low market price of cotton and the number of lynchings of black people (Beck and Tolnay, 1990). 'Strange Fruit', the timeless song performed by Billie Holiday and dealing with lynchings, sounds even more poignant when it is seen as the aggressive side-effect of economic frustration.

> Southern trees bear strange fruit,
> Blood on the leaves and blood at the root,
> Black bodies swinging in the southern breeze,
> Strange fruit hanging from the poplar trees.

Even minor frustrations can lead violence to erupt. We have noted the psychopath's indignation in response to minor frustrations, and noisy, crowded bars, for example, have been shown to be likely venues for violence (Clarke and Eck, 2003).

Obedience to authority, reaction to differences and frustration are all plausible features of the late Pleistocene human lifestyle. Other primate groups have leaders, neighbouring 'different' groups pose a threat, and frustration-driven aggression may be useful in extending one's foraging range at the expense of others. Readers are referred back to the website of the Evolution Institute, where many of the policy recommendations (e.g. in the collaborative design of local parks) seem to represent attempts to reduce frustration-instigated aggression in securing peaceful co-existence. In the same vein, mainstream situational crime prevention measures, for example in advocating well-organised pubs where people are served quickly and in order, may address and seek to remedy the evolutionary link between frustration and aggression. We feel the ghost of Stephen Jay Gould at our shoulder, muttering 'just-so stories'.

Is human violence special?

Human violence is unique until chimpanzees acquire nuclear weapons. Human violence is now unique because it can be done impersonally and at a distance. A drone can be launched by remote control at a target thousands of miles away where the person who guides it knows nothing and sees little of the people it will blow to bits. We are apes whose personality was shaped in times when to kill you had to be close enough to your victim to hear her screams and be splattered with her blood. Is our inner demon like those of the species most closely related to us? In this section, we will look at human violence by comparison with our primate relatives.

Until relatively recently, evolutionary explanations for violence have at best been misrepresented or over-simplified, and at worst (and arguably more frequently) dismissed or ignored. Some have rather bafflingly taken an opposite perspective, preferring to blame evolutionary theory for all that is wrong with human beings. Singling out evolutionary theory as the villain of the piece neither explains the totality of violence nor exculpates those who are violent – and does little to make it go away. In a newspaper article a few years ago, the journalist told how a 'creationist group' explicitly laid blame for all violence in the world (along with many other social ills) firmly at the door of Charles Darwin and his theory of evolution; considering him, and his theory, to be 'literally' responsible for the 'Descent of man' (and woman, we presume).

> For the creationist movement, it must have been the most miraculous of coups. The British venue for an assault on the theory of evolution was none other than the prestigious hall bearing Charles Darwin's name, built on the grounds of his former London home. . . . The speakers, Oktar Babuna and Ali Sudan, represent Harun Yahya, a creationist organisation which claims that there was no Stone Age, that God taught parrots to talk and that Darwinism is the root of all terrorism and must be eliminated.
>
> (Ian Sample, *Guardian*, Saturday 23 February 2008, p. 20)

In his 1966 book, *On aggression*, Konrad Lorenz explained aggression as an instinct which ensures the survival of the individual, group or species (Lorenz, 1966). Lorenz described animals (including humans) as innately aggressive but this is, as we have stressed, too simple. Rhesus monkeys do not attack other monkeys if a dominant, high-ranking monkey is present (Delgado, 1971) and bonobos prefer to resolve disputes peacefully (de Waal, 1989). Perhaps the most important point that Lorenz made about humans is that their physical feebleness means that there are no ritualised gestures of submission to limit the degree of harm done. Wolves, for example, submit by showing their throat, causing the dominant animal to cease an attack. Killing an adversary is disadvantageous to the group, since they hunt in packs. Natural selection has operated to make aggressors responsive to the postures of others, e.g. cats often arch their backs and howl (for what in the middle of the night seems hours) before any fighting occurs. People (until they had weapons usable at a distance) were relatively incapable of dealing death by their natural weapons, so lacked the self-limiting aggression of other animals.

Some claim this is too narrow a view of the use of violence and aggression in the animal world and look to evidence of violence in other primates to explain the human impulse to violence.

> The presence of deliberate chimpicide in our chimpanzee cousins raises the possibility that the forces of evolution, not just the idiosyncrasies of a

particular human culture, prepared us for violence. And the ubiquity of violence in human societies throughout history and prehistory is a stronger hint that we are so prepared.

(Pinker, 2002, p. 316)

Pinker cites factors such as large human upper body mass, the emotion of anger (and the existence of a word for it), fight or flight reactions to danger (autonomic nervous system responses) and brain trauma patients who have become violent as a consequence of frontal lobe damage, as evidence of human 'violence by design' (Pinker, 2002). He describes these factors (with the exception of the case of brain trauma patients) as universal, shared by all humans.

Unsurprisingly, evolutionists have situated explanations for why human beings display violence within a frame of natural and sexual selection. Both constitute competition for survival and reproduction, which means doing whatever is necessary to survive long enough to propagate genes. You will hopefully recall the distinction between replicator (gene) and survival vehicle (organism) which we made earlier. Sexual competition is more acute for males as they are concerned with quantity (have sex with as many females as possible and at least some of the offspring will be yours) and females with quality (selecting those males most likely to provide crucial parental investment to ensure, as best they can, that their shared young survive and flourish).[3] Other humans (with the exclusion of kin or collaborators eliciting at least weak altruism) constitute rivals to be manipulated or eliminated (Pinker, 2002). Sociobiologists open up Lorenz's argument by focusing on diverse ways in which individuals maximise the chances of their genes featuring in generations to come (S. Jones, 2000). 'Diverse ways' comprise all human behaviour which is analysed according to its functional advantage in spreading genes. Functional advantage includes violence *under some circumstances*.

In his classic *Biological bases of human social behaviour* (Hinde, 1974), Robert Hinde proposes 'a variety of evolutionary reasons why both the frequency of aggressive episodes, and the violence within them, should be minimized' (Hinde, 1974, p. 269). These include:

1   Both participants in an aggressive encounter are likely to be hurt. An individual up against insuperable odds does better to submit or try elsewhere. But it is also better for the potential winners of aggressive interactions to avoid them if they can, for combat brings risk of injury to both parties.
2   Excessive aggression can lead to the neglect of such activities as courtship, or feeding and rearing the young.
3   Excessive aggression may expose the aggressor to predation.
4   Hostility may be diverted toward unrecognised relatives, and thereby affect their reproductive success and thus the replacement of common genes.

Hinde suggests that one obvious way that violence is reduced involves the 'use of threat postures instead of actual combat' (1974, p. 269). Violence is also reduced by various social systems; as we shall see hierarchies presumably exist to minimise violence within the group. It has been consistently found animal and human violence is usually less between known individuals (Hinde, 1974).

The elephant in the room

We have left the most dramatic and important fact about violence until the end. You will recall that Stephen Pinker in 2002 wrote about the evolutionary origins of the capacity for violence. In 2011 he published a huge book which demonstrated that human violence has decreased dramatically over time (Pinker, 2011). The evidence is drawn from a wide range of sources and is irrefutable, though the residue of current violence is still enormous. This decline will not be a surprise to those criminologists who have bothered to study the subject, and it may irritate scholars like Ted Robert Gurr whose painstaking work over many years (Gurr, 1981) has been eclipsed by the Pinker book.[4] Pinker writes:

> the mind staggers to comprehend with deepening horror as it comes to realise just how much suffering has been inflicted by the naked ape upon its own kind. . . . [Y]et that species has also found ways to bring the numbers down, and allow a greater and greater proportion of humanity to live in peace and die of natural causes.
>
> (p. 696)

Why is the Pinker book so important? It is written by an evolutionist who acknowledged and studied the ubiquity of the human capacity for violence. It demonstrates that evolution has not sentenced us to a violent way of life. We earlier quoted E. O. Wilson's pithy comment that 'genes hold culture on a leash'(E O. Wilson, 1978). The decline in violence shows just how long that leash can be.

So what are the changes over time which have brought about the reduction in violence? Pinker identifies six major contributing trends. The first, which he terms the *Pacification Process*, reflects the transition of *Homo sapiens* from hunter-gatherer to farmer. This reduced the chronic raiding and feuding arising from fluidity of territorial ranges. The second change yielding reduced violence was termed the *Civilising Process* and involved the consolidation of patchworks of feudal territories into larger units with centralised authority and a commercial infrastructure. Third came the *Humanitarian Revolution*, moving to abolish socially sanctioned violence such as torture and slavery. The fourth major transition, the *Long Peace*, was reflected in the increased reluctance of major powers to wage 'hot' wars with each other. The fifth trend claimed by Pinker, the *New Peace*, is based upon his analysis that 'since the end of the Cold War in 1989, organised conflicts of all kinds . . . have declined throughout the world' (p. xxiv). Finally, the *Rights Revolution* comprises increasing revulsion against violence towards women, children, homosexuals and animals.

The trend that Pinker regards as pre-eminent seems to be the *Civilising Process*. Towards the end of his book he writes:

> A state that uses a monopoly on force to protect its citizens from one another may be the most consistent violence-reducer that we have encountered. . . . Pockets of anarchy that lay beyond the reach of government retained their violent cultures of honor, such as the peripheral and mountainous backwaters of Europe.
>
> (p. 680–681)

Chapter summary and reprise

This chapter has claimed the capacity for violence to be ubiquitous in humans, but the expression of violence to be very limited relative to the capacity. Individual differences in propensity to violence exist, one of particular interest being the discovery of gene–environment interactions whose continued existence has a plausible evolutionary basis. Difference between perpetrator and target, obedience to authority, and frustration (sometimes for trivial reasons) are flagged as promoters of violence. Most important, the amount of violence globally has decreased dramatically over time, with six reasons being presented as possible causes of the decline, the most important being the legal imposition of common standards of interpersonal behaviour by central governments.

6　Crime

It's a man thing?

Introduction

We have managed with some difficulty to keep gender issues on the margins of the discussion so far, but gender must now take centre stage, as it merits in discussions of crime. Robert Wright (1994) asserts that the leading cause of violence is maleness, which is pretty meaningless until one unpacks what it is about maleness that precipitates violence, as Wright seeks to do. However you measure it, men feature more amongst the ranks of officially processed offenders. During the second half of the twentieth century, conventional wisdom among criminologists was that this imbalance was a consequence of gender inequality across the board. Women were denied opportunities in crime as they were elsewhere. If they committed crime, male chivalry saw to it that they were not brought to book. One of the signs that equality had been achieved was to have been equal representation of women found guilty of crime. This has not happened. Nor has the gender gap narrowed over time in the relevant criminal statistics. For sure, equality has not been achieved but the direction of travel is clear, and this has not been reflected in statistics of criminality. Must we be driven to conclude that the gender gap is here to stay, and is a consequence of something more fundamental? Let's discuss sexual politics, Darwin style.

Mummy's baby, Daddy's maybe

To reiterate a point made more than once in the preceding pages, fitness in Darwinian terms means maximising the number of offspring brought to reproductive age. The human (man or woman) is the survival vehicle for the replicator gene. This makes for an obvious difference by gender in possible strategies to maximise fitness. Biology has imposed a limit on the number of babies a woman can have during her reproductive life. Menarche begins and menopause ends her fertile life an average of thirty-five years later. The limit is further reduced by declining fertility as she ages and her diminished fertility whilst breast-feeding (contraceptive amenorrhea). Moreover, the human child, with its uniquely long period of dependency, imposes massive time penalties on the primary caregiver, typically the mother. Cranium size in human neonates is so large that it imposes substantial risk of injury to the mother. Motherhood hurts. In stark contrast, male fertility is effectively limited only by the rate at which the male can impregnate women and his eventual death or impotence. This leads women who are prudent (in evolutionary terms, not necessarily in terms of personal fulfilment) to seek out a partner who will stay the course with her, contributing to the rearing of children until they reach adulthood. Males have two strategies open to them, often referred to as 'cads or dads' strategies (Cashdan, 1993). Cads seek to impregnate as widely as possible, making no contribution to child-rearing. Dads stay with the woman or women with whom they have conceived children. Cads will be the more effective survival vehicles if more of their children survive and reproduce. Otherwise the genes of Dads win out in the next generation.

The difference between men and women in their roles as survival vehicles has profound implications, not least for crime. In its crudest terms, it makes mothers vulnerable to abuse by their partners in their struggle to bring children to adulthood while retaining male support. Why did women need men? Anne Campbell looked at the literature and sees evidence that it was as calorie supplier rather than bodyguard (Campbell, 2012). In short, men did most of the hunting. Meat was the most calorie-intensive food around. Lactation required a good supply of calories.

As for men, *some* cohabiting males are careless or abusive towards their cohabitee's children by previous partners, so as to secure the longest possible remainder of her fertile years in which to bring up *their* offspring. We will deal with evidence in respect of the second crime risk first.

Among primate species, infanticide by immigrant males is a real and lethal threat accounting for more than a third of infant deaths (Smuts, 1992). If a criminologist has heard of just one phenomenon revealed by Darwinian theory, it will almost certainly concern the abuse and murder of step-children. Margo Wilson and Martin Daly have looked at violence (among other things) from a Darwinian standpoint for some thirty years. Their work provides an illustration of what (to restate a theme of Chapter 1) is the core idea in this book, namely that evolutionary insights lead you to ask different kinds of question. The notion that your own family represents the greatest danger to your health and your life was standard fare in the 1960s, and that undifferentiated view is still held in some quarters to this day. Daly and Wilson pointed to the malign reputation of step-parents in folklore and fairy stories. It was obvious to them that biological and step-parents should be separated in any analysis of abuse, (including lethal abuse) of children. They were somewhat cutting in their observations that social scientists had hitherto not bothered to look at the data in this way. They found that rates of child homicide by step-parents were greater by *one hundred times or more* than rates of child homicide by natural parents. In a nod to the fairy stories which demonised step-parents, they called this the Cinderella effect (Daly and Wilson, 1998). It is crucially important *not* to demonise step-parents generally. First, Daly and Wilson do not argue that killing the offspring of males who came before you (no pun intended) is adaptive, as it arguably is amongst lions and langurs. Rather they argue that care is given preferentially to one's own children. Abuse and homicide are outliers in the distribution of degrees to which this is so in individual cases. Most step-parents, despite occasional difficulties, do a fine job. They don't keep their daughters from going to balls or feed them poisoned apples. The son of one of the writers is a step-father. He and his step-daughter could not have a more loving relationship. But the Cinderella effect is real.

The Cinderella research has been much criticised, with Daly and Wilson defending their position persuasively (Daly and Wilson, 2007). They assert:

> Abundant confirmatory research has followed, such that the disproportionate victimisation of stepchildren is now the most extensively documented generalisation in the family violence literature. This ... raises further questions, such as what explains variability in the magnitude of Cinderella effects between maltreatment types and locales, and whether the individual level predictors of abuse are the same for fathers, mothers, step-fathers and step-mothers. Unfortunately, progress on these important issues has been hindered by a relentless distraction: the manufacture of 'controversy' about whether Cinderella effects exist at all. We suspect that the reason for this nay-saying resides largely, though not entirely, in antipathy to the Darwinian world-view and its application to Homo sapiens.
>
> (p. 383–384)

Consistent with a point we made in the opening chapter, Daly and Wilson (2007) write thus of their critics:

> From the perspective of two researchers on the receiving end of these attacks, a disturbing and sometimes perplexing element has been their incivility. . . . [Our critics] are not just sceptical, they are angry, and we are still not entirely sure what they are angry about.
>
> (p. 396)

The Cinderella effect is certainly the best known example of an evolution-inspired major finding applicable to crime and criminality. Less work has been done on the circumstances surrounding the situation where the baby is not the child of the male caregiver in the home. It is in the mother's best interests, if she wishes to retain her partner's support, not to acknowledge the possibility that the child is not his. At this stage we must mention Robert Trivers' theory of deceit and self-deception (Trivers, 2011). This fascinating theory is that deception is common in nature (think cuckoos and other parasitic birds adopting features of their victim species, and hoverflies adopting the stripes of more dangerous insects). When it comes to people, Trivers sees self-deception as a route to more effective deception of others. If one is sincere in one's erroneous belief, one will be more persuasive to others. You probably don't believe this. We do. Please read Trivers' brilliant book. The relevance of the Trivers thesis to the situation of uncertain paternity can be introduced by a joke about a famous soccer player whose name is omitted here. The player (allegedly) committed adultery, his wife becoming aware of the relationship. At about the same time, his wife fell pregnant. The player looked worried. His wife asked him what the problem was. He said 'I was having sex with you and another woman. How do I know the baby's yours?' The joke is funny (if it is) because there is for all practical purposes never any doubt who a child's biological mother is, but there is about the father. In an estimated 5–10 per cent of cases, an infant's father is not the mother's partner. At birth, women present are much more likely to remark on the baby's resemblance to the *father* than to the mother (Daly and Wilson, 1982). As Mark Pagel puts it, the women are reassuring the man that he really is the father. The baby 'colludes' with that impression. For example 'the blond hair and blue eyes so common in Caucasian infants disappear in most of them around the second birthday' (p. 316) when the acute need for a second caregiver has waned somewhat (Pagel, 2012). The recent advent of DNA paternity testing will certainty cause conflict between partners, both when the father is shown not to be the partner and when the mother considers her partner's request for a test indicates a lack of trust.

Our discussion of the Cinderella effect and paternity ambiguity came early in this chapter because of how well known this work is, relative to other work in the area. But we must now step back to the most dramatic fact about crime with which we started the chapter, namely that everywhere and everywhen, males seem to commit more of it than females. The same factors seem to yield high or low rates of crime in a society or epoch, i.e. males and females appear to dance to the same environmental tune, crime-wise, but men always seem to commit more (Campbell, 1999). Choose any area of the world and choose any historical time period for it and you will find that men typically account for at least 80 per cent of all crime (Ayres and Murray, 2005; Heidensohn, 2002). As noted earlier, it is now common for social scientists (the gender gap having failed to narrow with the consequent implausibility of the view that gender inequality was mirrored in unequal representation among processed offenders), in their attempt to answer the question 'why more male crime?', to have recourse to the 'differential socialisation' of men and women (Wortley, 2010).

But let us look at the facts before socialisation. The sex-linked chromosomes in a normal human male are labelled XY. In a normal human female they are XX. But the Y chromosome now carries only 86 genes compared to about 2,000 on the X chromosome. Why is the Y chromosome so small? Please take a break and look at a relevant demonstration.[1] If you are male, you may cringe at the notion of rotting Y chromosomes, but please persist, it's very informative. The romantic image of man and woman cooperating to make a baby is belied by the conflict between the sperm and ovum delegated to do the business at the sharp end of development. Anne Campbell's recent book is remorselessly clear on this and many other topics, and should be required reading for anyone interested in gender and evolution (Campbell, 2012). The best image of the genetics of reproduction by sex is that of an arms race as male and female attempt to out-manoeuvre one another.

At the chromosomal level, XX is the winner. But the victory stops there. To take one rather dreadful example of gender inequality relevant to differences in adult populations by gender, even now countries differ greatly in the relative proportions of male and female infants who do not reach their fifth birthday.[2] Whatever it is that leads more girls in some countries to die as babies, it certainly imposes a selection pressure, which may well have been stronger in the past. Add to this the recent possibility of selective abortion by sex of foetus (Pinker, 2011). Taken together and stated crudely, the population of girls who survive to be socialised is a selected group.

> Differential gender mortality has been a documented problem for decades and led to reports in the early 1990s of 100 million 'missing women' across the developing world. . . . The large cohorts of 'surplus' males now reaching adulthood are predominantly of low socioeconomic class, and concerns have been expressed that their lack of marriageability, and consequent marginalization in society, may lead to antisocial behavior and violence, threatening societal stability and security.
>
> (Hesketh and Xing, 2006, p. 13271)

Probably the best, and best known, attempt to account for gender differences in criminality is Anne Campbell's 'Staying Alive' theory (Campbell, 1999). It centres on aggression and deserves extensive mention. It does not let patriarchy off the hook and provides a fine example of an evolutionary account with feminist sensibilities about what should be done in policy terms.

Campbell's starting point is fourfold.

1   Human males engage in more aggression than females from about the age of two years onwards.
2   The sex differential increases with the seriousness of the aggression.
3   There is a high correlation between rates of male and female aggression across geographical areas.
4   There is a high correlation of male and female aggression across age (i.e. the age–crime curve is similar for both sexes).

She contends that maternal presence is more important than paternal presence for offspring survival, therefore natural selection would favour women who place a higher premium on survival. This accounts for greater female risk-averseness and fearfulness in situations which threaten physical harm. A mother can be sure that her baby carries 50 per cent of her genes. A father cannot, despite the assurances of resemblance we mentioned earlier. So there is a higher premium placed on infant survival among mothers than among (putative) fathers.

Campbell contends:

> Sex differences in aggression can be traced ultimately to sex differences in parental investment. Higher variance in reproductive success in men, resulting from lower parental investment, creates incentives for competition to achieve intrasexual dominance, while women's greater investment and role in caring for offspring creates costs for dangerous confrontations. Data suggest that, at

a proximal psychological level, sex differences in fear, but not anger, mediate involvement in aggression.[3]

Women mourn their dead babies more profoundly than do men. The greater threat to child survival of maternal death has been observed in at least one surviving hunter-gatherer society (the Ache of Paraguay). Sensation seeking is taken to be the opposite of fear and males show greater levels of sensation seeking. The strongest predictor of elective preventive health care is gender. Women estimate the danger of the same aggressive encounter more highly than do men. Girls' aggression takes more covert and less physically dangerous forms. Women aggress for resources rather than status. When asked for accounts of their violence, women tend to excuse rather than justify. Taken together, Campbell has collected an impressive array of facts consistent with her notion of female violence. Campbell (with Catherine Cross) draws attention to one fact which sits uneasily with survival theory: the roughly equal frequency of aggressive acts directed at intimate partners. They argue that fear reduction in women necessary to permit sexual intimacy, possibly mediated by oxytocin, also diminishes women's normal restraint on aggressive behaviour.

In a longer book than this, one concentrating on the biological underpinnings of cooperation, oxytocin would merit a chapter of its own. Variously known as the 'cuddle chemical' or the 'love chemical', it seems to reduce shyness and increase trust. It is probably fundamental to the establishment of cooperation and pro-social behaviour.

We have discussed female aggression moderated by the need to survive. Female mate selection is a means whereby a woman seeks partially to pre-empt the survival problem. Striving for wealth, a good job and status are known to attract women and therefore are likely to result in reproductive success (Buss, 1994). We are reminded of the spoof chat-show character Mrs Merton (played by Caroline Aherne) who once asked the 'lovely, lovely Debbie McGee' what it was that first attracted her to the millionaire Paul Daniels!

We have discussed female violence. We now turn to the relative numbers of men and women in a population, and the crime problems this might pose. In their seminal 1983 book *Too many women?* Marcia Guttentag and Paul Secord provide a compelling argument that in any given society, the 'sex ratio' (number of males to females) has important social consequences. The level of violence (particularly homicide rates) in any society, at any time, is directly attributable to the ratio of males to females (Daly and Wilson, 1988). A short supply of women (the wording is offensive; women are not a commodity) can have a negative effect as it increases competition between men and levels of violence increase as a consequence. Domestic violence increases as men fight to gain and keep reproductive access to scarce females, or form groups of 'bare branch' misbehaving men who have failed to mate (Pinker, 2011). An 'oversupply' of women results in women having 'a subjective sense of powerlessness' and feeling 'devalued by the society ... devalued as mere sex objects' (Guttentag and Secord, 1983, p. 20) as men, presumably, are more likely to have sexual relationships outside of, and in addition to, marriage. The implications of gender-skewed abortion and the differential rates of neonatal mortality mentioned above have serious, as yet unknown, implications for crime.

Something which we find mind-blowing and impossible to explain in any non-evolutionary terms is the excess of male births which occur during and after wars. This happened before sex-specific abortion became possible and allowed son preference to distort things (Hesketh and Xing, 2006). Some deep and subtle mechanism, which would have been useful to hunter-gatherer groups, increases the proportion of male births after male numbers have been depleted by conflict. We distort sex ratios of births at our peril.

And now for men

Males account for most crime. The age–crime relationship shows that most crime is committed by young men. The prevalence of male violence in a society seems to be influenced by natural and sexual selection pressures, with males often competing violently with each other when females are found in less plentiful supply (Daly and Wilson, 1988; Kanazawa and Still, 2000). Male sexual jealousy is offered as an example of an evolved psychological mechanism, developed to solve the adaptive problem of paternal uncertainty (Daly *et al.*, 1982). Men who 'monopolise' women represent to other men obstacles which must be overcome by fair means or foul, with women representing a scarce reproductive commodity worth fighting for or overpowering. Some evolutionary psychologists point to 'polygyny' as the main agitator (see Box 6.1).

We have dealt with the implications of unbalanced sex ratios and the mysterious change in sex ratios of newborns after wars. We discussed the link between step-parenthood, child abuse and infanticide. We have dealt with the probable survival strategy of women, with the consequence of lower rates of overt violence. What else can we say about men? We have dealt too little with the crime-relevant details of sexual selection, to which may be added youth and unmarried status (see Mesquida and Wiener, 1996, 1999). Violence is often about sexual selection. Stressing the primacy of sexual selection as the root of frustration is the distinctive contribution of evolutionary thinking (Roach and Pease, 2011).

Male crime, in its entirety, has been explained by some evolutionary psychologists as the consequence of men trying to appropriate resources necessary to attract women. Kanazawa and Still suggest that in relation to property crime in general, this is the primary causal factor. A student project is waiting in which this is tested by showing that the objects which younger men choose to steal and retain for their own use are primarily items of display (clothes, jewellery) or the means to obtain them (money). 'Material resources in traditional societies, however, tend to be concentrated in the hands of elder men. Younger men are often excluded from attaining them through legitimate means and must therefore resort to illegitimate means' (Kanazawa and Still, 2000, p. 440).

Sociologists have long since identified both stifled aspirations and limited life opportunities as correlates of male crime, particularly that committed by young

---

Box 6.1   Polygyny and homicide

Polygyny refers to having more than one mate. Human evolutionary history has often seen men have multiple mates (simultaneously or successively), often at the expense of those without (Daly and Wilson, 1988; Kanazawa and Still, 1999; Kanazawa, 2007). In their study of homicide, and who kills who, Daly and Wilson (1988) note that with some males monopolising other's access to females, reproduction becomes a highly intrasexual competitive game that can lead to a high level of violence (and homicide) between them. In this competitive light, violence can be seen as a means by which males overcome this obstacle. Daly and Wilson (1988) found that most homicides begin with a seemingly trivial dispute between males about *honour, status and reputation* (exemplified by the 'are you looking at my bird?' scenario), violent crime rates reflecting the ferocity of the competition. Evolutionary psychologists argue that the more polygynous the society, the more aggressive and violent the men (Daly and Wilson, 1988). Stephen Pinker suggests that this explains why men are the violent gender, and why they always have something to fight over, even when their survival needs have been met (Pinker, 2002).

---

males, who, as it has been well established, commit the bulk of crime in any society you might care to name (e.g. Merton, 1938). The 'age–crime curve' denotes that the relationship between age and crime is invariant across all social, historical and cultural contexts – in fact, across all conditions (Hirschi and Gottfredson, 1983). It's young men overwhelmingly who commit crime. Indeed Terrie Moffitt's typology distinguishes transient juvenile offending from life-course persistent offending, inviting the thought that the former is testosterone-fuelled theft to attract girls (see Box 6.2).

Crime provides for the adolescent and young adult male the necessary female attraction 'make-over'. Violence of course can, and is, often used to achieve this reproductive goal and is offered as reason why young males commit the bulk of crime across the world. Violence serves two functions; protecting male status and honour, or forcefully discouraging rivals from competition for mates (killing being permanent discouragement). Some boldly claim that rape is similarly explained, as the same psychological mechanism that compels men to compete in attracting women compels them to demand illegitimate access violently when their prospects are 'very dim' (Buss, 1994). Thornhill and Thornhill (1983) found in their study that predatory rapists were overwhelmingly men of lower status. But is this sufficient explanation for why males commit a vast majority of violent crime?

Social status as a predictor of violent male criminality including rape is not as clear-cut as some might suggest (e.g. Kanazawa, 2007). We must bear in mind that rich and powerful men possess the means necessary to 'buy their way out' of

---

**Box 6.2   Moffitt's developmental taxonomy
            (typology) of offenders**

In her *Developmental Taxonomy* Terrie Moffitt (1993,1994) attempts to
account for why some offenders desist from crime and others persist in
criminal activity and takes the aggregate age–crime curve (Hirschi and
Gottfredson, 1983) as a starting point. Two distinct groups of offenders are
identified, each influenced by a unique set of criminogenic and antisocial
factors, which extends over the individual's life.

The first group, referred to as *life-course persistent* offenders, is characterised by an early onset of crime, displaying active and persistent offending and showing crime versatility throughout the life-course. Such offenders
are explained as possessing 'inherited or acquired neuro-psychological variations' (Piquero and Moffitt, 2004, p. 179). Moffitt suggests that life-course
persistent offenders are pre-disposed to crime and anti-social behaviour as
a result of inherited and/or early acquired neuropsychological deficit
(Moffitt, 2003). The gene variant MOAO which lowers the activity of the
enzyme monoamine oxidase A and which seems implicated in violence is
identified as being of particular interest (Caspi *et al.*, 2002).

The second group (and the far larger of the two) comprises those
described as *adolescence limited offenders* – those who restrict their
offending to their adolescence (Piquero and Moffitt, 2004). Moffitt identifies
a maturity gap and peer social context as important factors underlying
adolescence-limited delinquency. Offending generally constitutes relatively
minor offences such as petty theft, low-level vandalism and minor road
traffic violations. In contrast to the life-course persistent group, because the
adolescence-limited group displays 'normal' pre-delinquent development,
most possess the characteristics and abilities necessary to desist from
offending as they move into adult roles, for example, the ability to form
good relationships and the cognitive skills required to begin a career.

Members of this group are usually able to return gradually to 'a more
conventional lifestyle' (Piquero and Moffitt, 2004). There can of course be
'snares' which delay or hamper a return to a conventional lifestyle, such as
receiving a criminal record, drug addiction and unwanted pregnancy.

---

charges and convictions, where their less affluent counterparts do not. So a
cautionary note is prudent. Rape cannot be seen simply as the remit of young and/
or powerless men with little other prospect of reproductive access. This would be
not just the gross oversimplification of a complex phenomenon but also grossly
unfair, since older men are also convicted, along with wealthy businessmen and
celebrities (for example, the former heavyweight world boxing champion 'Iron'
Mike Tyson). Also, if asked, most women would say that they find males who use
violence unattractive, so violence to attract mates appears counter-intuitive. Why

would violence be used by males to secure reproductive chances if it in fact had an adverse effect on those they seek to attract? It would be used to impregnate women, by the future discounting 'cads' strategy mentioned earlier.

Discounting time

So why is it that young males account for most of the crime in any country that you care to name, giving shape to one of criminology's most robust findings – the 'age–crime curve'?

The evolution-based answer, unsurprisingly, hinges around reproductive competition between males. If we think about it, reproducing in our teenage years runs the risk of a reduced chance of survival in terms of what a teenage parent can invest in and provide for their offspring (both materially and emotionally). Conversely, delaying reproduction until later runs a risk of it not happening at all. Dying before another reproductive opportunity might occur was a real concern for our ancestors, more so admittedly than for most of us today, but the crucial decision when to reproduce remains, at the subconscious level at least.

We pick up on how environments might inform 'time-discounting' perceptions in a later chapter.

To recap, thus far we have discussed how the evolutionary approach with its tenets of natural selection and sexual selection is useful when trying to develop a framework for explaining why crime (and violence) tend to be a male thing. We turn now to an evolution-focused discussion of an even more specific form of male dominated crime – gang violence.

Gangs

Palmer and Tilley empirically tested the hypothesis that sexual access to women was the primary motivation for males to join gangs (Palmer and Tilley, 1995). The motivation for their research was the rise of gang warfare, common around the world particularly in large cities in America such as New York and Los Angeles, where gang membership often resulted in death or serious injury. Palmer and Tilley wanted to know why males joined gangs where the risk of death was a distinct possibility. Their hypothesis was: to 'get girls'.

Palmer and Tilley (1995) compared a sample of fifty-seven reported gang members in Colorado Springs, Colorado, with sixty-three same-age, gang unaffiliated males from the same community. The 'gang member' sample reported an average of 1.67 sex partners during the past month, considerably higher than their 'non gang member' counterparts who reported 1.22 sex partners. Interestingly, the two participants with the highest number of sex partners were found to be the gang leaders, who reported having ten and eleven sex partners in the previous ninety days, respectively. None of the 'non gang member' group reported more than five sex partners over the same period. This led the researchers to conclude that being a member of a gang increased a male's reproductive access, especially if they were high up in the gang hierarchy.

A degree of caution must be exercised with regard to the findings of this study, particularly to the reliability of the reporting of number of sex partners by gang members. Nevertheless, the findings are interesting and they echo one of the main reasons for males engaging in warfare mooted by evolutionary psychologists: to increase reproductive opportunity. Chagnon, in his study of the Yanomamö, found that the most frequently cited explanation for going to war was revenge for a previous killing, and the most common cause of the initial fighting had been women, and those males that had killed most (of an opposing tribe) had had a higher number of sexual partners (cited in Buss, 2004, p. 304).

A somewhat pervasive explanation for why males join coalitions (often violent) is pursuit of increased reproductive access. Daly and Wilson's study of homicide, for example, found that most were accounted for as disputes between young males over a female (Daly and Wilson, 1988). We remind the reader that evolutionary explanation for such phenomena as why young males join violent coalitions operates on an 'ultimate goal' level (i.e. the underlying motivation is to replicate genes) and not at the proximal level (i.e. how that motivation manifests itself). The latter is the remit of mainstream criminology.

Having dealt with evolutionary explanations, we turn now to their structural and dispositional undergirding. Box 6.3 poses an interesting question.

Box 6.3   Boys will be boys

Those readers with male offspring (or those who have ever been boys themselves) will probably testify that boys play-fight from a very early age and often with little to model such seemingly 'aggressive' behaviour. Although only play-fighting, the inclination to demonstrate strength, courage and agility amongst peers appears innate. This is made even more disappointing when as a parent you have intervened to keep them from being aware of such beings as 'Power Rangers' and 'Teenage Mutant Ninja Turtles' and yet they still exhibit the same quasi-aggressive behaviour, seemingly conjured up from thin air. Why?

Are women more often empaths?

In Chapter 3 we identified the capacity for empathy or compassion to be a necessary condition of pro-social behaviour (along with ToM and sense of fairness), and described Simon Baron-Cohen's work on the topic. Before going on, it should be emphasised that the stress here on empathy is entirely compatible with other theories, such as the Campbell survival theory. The relationship might be as follows. More successful mothers (i.e. those who succeed in bringing their children to maturity, perhaps helped by their success in inducing male loyalty) have certain attributes. Empathy, which would entail (among other things) anticipating and defusing or deflecting adult male aggression from the child, would be a trait which was very useful in helping the mother's survival strategy to be effective. What follows should therefore be seen as elaborating a means to the evolutionary end we have described above. In that way it is equivalent to our earlier discussion of the empathy circuit in relation to the evidence of the relationship between empathy and pro-social behaviour. Looking into the brain only shows that the hardware is there to give effect to an evolved characteristic.

Baron-Cohen's 'empathising–systemising' (ES) theory posits a difference in empathising ability between male and female brains, with females on the whole better at empathising than males. ES theory is consistent with universal findings that men offend more than women.

Other questions about the relationship between empathy and crime remain to be answered. For example, do male offenders really have low empathy or do they have similar levels but counteract this by activating evolved mechanisms for neutralisation triggered by predictable environments, settings and situations? (Sykes and Matza, 1957; or see McLoughlin and Muncie, 2001, p. 186 for a brief synopsis of Sykes and Matza's theory).

It is not inconceivable that male brains hold different levels of both empathy and neutralisation; for example an individual with low empathy level who was thinking of offending would only need low neutralisation, whereas those with high empathy levels would need high neutralisation. This is speculation. Brain imaging work while making excuses has not featured in the literature of which we are aware. Research in this area holds big implications for those rehabilitative (correctional) programmes focused on offending behaviour. We are currently thinking of 'putting our money with where our mouths are' in conducting research focused on empathising and systemising levels in male and female offenders (imprisoned and in the community), but the results from this are for another day. Our sole objective with this chapter is to introduce the reader to the possibilities that taking a wider evolutionary perspective holds for understanding the evolved ability of empathy and its interaction with male and female offending patterns.

Chapter summary and reprise

Males commit much more crime than women. Evolutionary thinking suggests that this has much to do with differing routes to reproductive success. Women, it is suggested, place a premium on mate selection of those who are most likely to remain as carer during the period in which the child is dependent, and on ensuring that they survive to succour the child. Males, perhaps especially those displaying adolescent-limited criminality, see criminality as a means towards success in acquiring female sexual companionship. Those anticipating less material or economic success are prone to future discounting, whereby they maximise the number of impregnations and eschew a continuing role as nurturant father. Stress is laid upon the criminogenic consequences of unbalanced sex ratios in the population, and the danger posed to achieving balance by son preference and consequent foetal sex-based abortions.

7 Beyond the proximal

Evolution, environments and criminal behaviour

Introduction

Hopefully (if we have got it right) by this chapter, the reader is left in no doubt that the objective of this book has been to apply the evolutionary perspective to behaviour that we now deem pro-social, criminal or anti-social. Principally, we have sought to do this by suggesting that such behaviour proved adaptive in early ancestral environments (EEA) before written law. We have endeavoured to show how such behaviour could have originated and how it might have evolved in accordance with the process of natural and sexual selection. Criminal-like behaviour (there was no crime before law) represents tactics in the struggle for survival and reproductive access (i.e. gene replication). This leads many evolutionary psychologists to assert that, though morally repugnant, crime is at least *biologically normal* behaviour (e.g. Kanazawa, 2003). Such behaviour, it is argued, must have conferred some evolutionary advantage for our ancestors (Walsh and Ellis, 2007).

Against that, we have reported the work of sociobiologists and mathematicians who show beyond a doubt that as a species we are ultra-social, and our default setting is pro-social and cooperative. Serious criminality now is often contrastingly 'maladaptive' in the sense that there is nothing (short of capital punishment, suicide or exclusive homosexuality) like a long stretch in prison to curtail one's reproductive opportunities.

We are apes designed for an environmental niche far removed from the one most of us now inhabit. A crude analogy is provided by the battle tank. Set up for moving about Europe, it works most of the time. Transfer it for operations in the desert and it would quickly fail. It would overheat, sand would enter and grind away at exposed bearings, and so on. If it kept moving, it would be destroyed because its European camouflage colours would make it conspicuous in the desert. Tank speeds in desert battles need to be faster; in wooded areas speed is sacrificed by lower gearing to negotiate wooded and uneven terrain. People are also equipped for particular environmental niches. Natives of high altitude regions have distinctive oxygen metabolism (Gill and Pugh, 1964) and numerous other geographic variations in evolved behaviour have been documented (Foster and Endler, 1999). Skin colour became light as a result of the need to absorb more sunlight for vitamin D production as *Homo sapiens* moved north out of Africa. The current 'lifestyle diseases timebomb', including obesity, diabetes and many other disorders, is a consequence of the fact that the environment for which we were designed is no more (Gluckman and Hanson, 2006).

As such, put simply, evolved behaviour (including criminal) is always expressed according to what Walsh and Ellis (2007) refer to as 'current environmental circumstances'. How ancestrally originated behaviour transfers and manifests itself in the present depends on the environment and context in which it occurs. When the repertoire of cheating behaviours was limited (hide what you had foraged or hunted, hit your neighbour, seduce his partner) the scope for the free-rider was somewhat limited. Now the range is enormous. One too many electronic exchanges, a wealth of things to steal, a complex financial system to undermine and defraud. All these possibilities tip things in favour of the free-rider. This provides all the more reason to buttress the evolved default position, cooperation, and to deny whatever crime opportunities we can.

In this chapter we suggest that although much attention in crime reduction is quite rightly placed on the more immediate causes of crime (referred to as *proximal* causes hereafter), for example 'situational theories', or on the causes of individual propensities for criminal behaviour (referred to as *developmental and learning factors* hereafter) such as 'poor parenting' or economic inequality, there is a trick being missed. The addition of an evolution-informed criminological approach would enable us to consider how more distant ultimate causes of natural and sexual selection (hereafter referred to as *distal factors*) contribute to, and interact with, proximal and developmental/learning factors when explaining criminal behaviour. Commonly referred to as Gene × Environment (G×E) effects, these are illustrated by Caspi and colleagues' wonderful example of the interaction between expression of the MAOA gene and violent behaviour (Caspi *et al.*, 2002), as discussed in an earlier chapter. Figure 7.1 illustrates how the three interact.

A focus on the proximal causes of crime is a focus on the 'here and now', i.e. the immediate situation. What is it about an environment such as a bar or a shop which makes it conducive to crime and attractive for criminal behaviour? This type of question is common when trying to determine the proximal reasons why specific crime is occurring in a specific place, at a specific time. Environmental criminology, for example, looks for proximal causes of crime by focusing on environments and how they might 'cause' (or at least facilitate) crime commission. At face value, there appears little point in applying an evolutionary criminology approach here as we assume for example that a male burglar does not consciously think about how his ill-gotten gains can be used to improve his chances of securing a mate with whom to reproduce and so replicate his genes. If romance wasn't dead already, then accept our apologies if we have just killed it.

We do not dispute the importance of 'opportunity' in the commission of crime, indeed both of us have spent many an hour devising and evaluating environmental modifications and interventions with which to reduce specific crime opportunities. Our point of departure from most viewpoints is perhaps one more of focus than conflict. We believe that additional questions need to be addressed which go to the

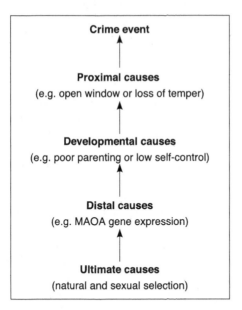

Figure 7.1   Ultimate to proximal causes of crime.

heart of individuals' search for crime opportunities, and how they recognise and select amongst those which are present in the first place. This is no small consideration if trying to understand crime commission and to block the opportunities for it. Take for example leaving a window open in an empty car, which can either be interpreted as a logical thing to do on a warm day (apologies to our fellow British readers here who will have to use their imaginations about hot weather) or conversely, illogical because it provides a five star opportunity for somebody to commit a crime (e.g. steal the car and/or the laptop computer which is in full view on the rear seat). In this chapter we try to tease out what exactly it is about certain environments that shouts out loud to some, 'crime opportunity, come take me', whilst for most it remains silent. The question we explore is the extent to which an individual recognises crime opportunities through learning and what degree is attributable to some hardwired psychological mechanisms forged by evolution which we all share.

We begin by exploring how the *environmental criminology* approach focuses on the immediate here and now – how proximal settings cause and facilitate crime commission, before introducing the concept of *affordance*, which is simply those actions which come to mind in a certain setting, thus providing a tangible link between individual and setting in the commission of crime. Next, we look at how evolved 'hardwired' psychological mechanisms influence crime affordance in modern environments and settings, by first looking at how evolutionary psychologists have found the existence of innate preferences for specific landscapes and habitats in the wiring of the human brain, before moving to discussion of how this might influence criminal and anti-social behaviour, using the example of young males who discount time and take risks in response to certain environmental cues (e.g. low life expectancy). Lastly, we complete the circle by suggesting that Gene × Environment (G×E) interactions best demonstrate how evolutionary 'ultimate causes' influence the 'proximal causes' involved with criminal behaviour.

Proximal causes of crime or 'opportunity knocks'

> There's a lot of opportunities
> If you know when to take them.
>
> (Pet Shop Boys: 'Opportunities')

The Compact Oxford Dictionary defines an opportunity as 'a favourable time or set of circumstances for doing something'. The key words are favourable (one presumes at least for the main actor) and circumstances. Crime opportunities are therefore times and settings favourable to crime, such as an open window in a car, walking down a dark alley, or observing someone's PIN whilst waiting at an ATM. What is certain is that such opportunities are only opportunities if they are perceived to be by the individual in question. Whether they are realised and acted upon is another question entirely and is usually explained away by criminologists as 'criminal propensity' (i.e. the mysterious inclination to give in to temptation and act criminally). What is of interest here is not so much propensity (its importance we have discussed in depth elsewhere) but how individuals are able to perceive opportunities as 'opportunities' and this is neglected in most criminology texts.

The importance of opportunity in crime commission is obvious; without it even the most criminal of us would struggle to commit any sort of crime. For example, how can you commit murder without access to a victim, or commit burglary without a building to burgle? One wonders just how many women Peter Sutcliffe (aka the Yorkshire Ripper) did not attack because he felt the right opportunity had not presented itself? How many passers-by unconsciously saved women by appearing unexpectedly just as he prepared to attack? Indeed, many a crime mystery novel plot revolves around the twin concerns of the suspect's opportunity and motive to commit the crime (read any Agatha Christie novel if you don't believe us).

The importance of the role of opportunity in crime commission is best summarised by Felson and Clarke's (1998) claim that 'opportunity makes the thief', with temptation one assumes a willing partner in crime. In an approach to understanding crime such as this, proximal causes are of primary concern and the modification of environments (e.g. better lit streets) to reduce opportunities for crime is seen as key to reducing crime overall. This is the mantra of *environmental criminology*.

Environmental criminology

> Environmental criminology is a family of theories that share a common interest in criminal events and the immediate circumstances in which they occur.
>
> (Wortley and Mazerolle, 2008, p. 1)

Environmental criminology differs from more mainstream criminology in that it views crime as an event which must be understood as 'confluences of offenders, victims, targets and laws, in specific settings at specific places and times' (Brantingham and Brantingham, 1991, p. 2). Environmental criminologists look for crime patterns which they seek to explain in terms of environmental influences (Wortley and Mazerolle, 2008). It is the environment in which a crime occurs that is considered most important when trying to understand and prevent it. Environmental criminology's perspective on crime contrasts most noticeably with more traditional criminology in that it purposely chooses not to seek to explain how biological, developmental and social factors conspire to produce criminality. Instead, as discussed previously, it is simply that 'opportunity makes the thief' (Felson and Clarke, 1998). As we are clearly not all thieves despite numerous opportunities on a daily basis to be so, opportunity cannot be considered as sole explanation for theft any more than for other crimes. Perhaps 'opportunity makes the theft more likely' is nearer the mark and is a lot less controversial.

To be fair, most environmental criminologists do say that 'inclination' is needed, but do not care to elaborate. They see no need, since crime is the object of interest, not criminality (i.e. not what led the individual to offend in the first place). Environmental criminologists are more concerned with what the current dynamics of a crime are. For example, where did it happen? Who was involved? How did they do it? (Wortley and Mazerolle, 2008). Put bluntly, it is about preventing crime, not about how individuals become criminal and even less about reforming or 'curing' offenders. Criminals are so inclined for whatever reason – end of story.

Before we examine in more detail the environmental criminology mantra that it is proximal (immediate) environments which are most important to understanding crime, it is worthwhile spending a little time exploring the cornerstones of the environmental criminological approach, namely the Routine Activity Approach, the Rational Choice Perspective and Crime Pattern Theory. All of these to some extent focus on the interaction between individual and environment when trying to explain crime.

Routine Activity Theory

Arguably, the theoretical approach in criminology that has most strongly advocated the importance in crime causation of the intersection of individual and setting is the routine activity approach (Cohen and Felson, 1979; Felson, 1994). In routine activities, the convergence of three elements – a motivated offender, a suitable victim or target and (the absence of) a capable guardian – results in a crime (see Clarke and Eck, 2005 for an excellent summary).

With this approach the principle focus is on the settings for crime, not the offender. It is predominantly about how different types of environment or setting influence the occurrence of crime, rather than about how types of individuals intersect with types of settings to create specific acts of crime (Wikström, 2005). For example, one focus is what makes good targets of opportunity, and not how the offender got to be motivated, variations in degree of motivation, or how motivation intersects with the situational features present (Pease, 2006, p. 56).

Routine Activity Theory (RAT) has been supplemented by related perspectives such as Brantingham and Brantingham's (1993) Crime Pattern Theory and has influenced understanding of the importance of the role of settings and environments in crime causation by contending that crime rates are best regarded as the unwanted consequence of routine everyday life (Pease, 2006). Changes in routine play a significant role in determining the types of settings in which crime occurs (Wikström, 2005). Burglary, for example, was seen to rise in America in the 1960s, as a consequence of women beginning to enter the workforce for the first time in large numbers. More women at work meant fewer 'capable guardians' at home, translating to more opportunities for burglars to burgle (Cohen and Felson, 1979; Felson, 1994). Felson also addresses issues such as the widening gap between sexual maturity and economic independence as a factor inclining to crime (i.e. economic independence now comes much later in life, if indeed it comes at all). An observation which (as we have seen in earlier chapters) is consistent with the evolutionary approach, albeit unwittingly.

But although the routine activity approach has concentrated on the supply of criminal opportunities (the role of settings especially) and the role of general social factors in determining 'motivated offenders', it has rather neglected the role of individual differences between offenders, and neither has it sought the mechanisms through which, at the point of intersection of individual and setting, individuals are moved to commit acts of crime (Wikström, 2005; Pease, 2006). Attempts to link the theory to *Control Theories* (Hirschi, 1986; Hirschi and Gottfredson, 1988; Gottfredson and Hirschi, 1990, 2003) and *Rational Choice Theory* (Cornish and Clarke, 1986; Clarke and Felson, 1993), although acknowledged, have so far mostly been a question of saying that it is a good idea and that they are complementary, rather than saying how they could and should be integrated (Wikström, 2005, p. 214).

Rational Choice Theory

Cornish and Clarke (2008) differentiate their rational choice perspective from others:

> Instead of viewing criminal behaviour as the outcome of stable criminal motivations, it views the desires, preferences and motives of offenders and potential offenders as similar to those of the rest of us, and as in continual interaction with contemporary opportunities and constraints to produce, reinforce and sometimes reduce criminal behaviours.
>
> (Cornish and Clarke, 2008, p. 21)

Their rational choice perspective is very much centred in the here and now, as is wider environmental criminology. It is about the influence of the current environment on behaviour and environmental/learning theory (Cornish and

Clarke, 2008). Clarke and Cornish (1983 - reproduced in Cornish and Clarke, 2008) list four main elements of their approach, summarised below.

1   While an individual's emotional inheritance and upbringing play some part in delinquency, the major determinants are those provided by the current environment.
2   The current environment provides the cues and stimuli for delinquency as well as the reinforcements.
3   Since delinquent acts are learned in particular environments, they will be repeated under closely similar conditions. Consistencies in behaviour over time are therefore dependent on consistencies in environments.
4   Delinquent acts of different kinds do not serve equivalent functions for the actor; each is acquired and maintained by situational variables specific to it, and it alone. This is not to deny, however, that some individuals, by virtue of their particular circumstances, may learn a range of delinquent behaviours.

Cornish and Clarke demonstrate the importance that environmental criminology places on environment and setting as opposed to the seemingly deliberate neglect of the origins of criminal propensity, and this has led some to accuse supporters of the rational choice perspective of taking a 'cardboard cut-out' view of the offender (Ekblom, 2007). Although to be fair to Cornish and Clarke, they do describe it as an evolving approach and modify it periodically in light of constructive feedback (e.g. Wortley, 2001). As emphasis is with environment rather than offender propensity, the perspective promotes the idea of crime as an *event* that offenders make decisions in relation to, since offenders 'will concentrate solely on those situational factors that hinder or advance instrumental action in fulfilment of the criminal goal' (Cornish and Clarke, 2008, p. 31). The 'crime as an event' approach has led Cornish (1994) to produce complex crime *scripts* designed to help identify every stage of 'the crime commission process', the decisions and actions that must be taken at each stage and the necessary resources (e.g. suitable locations) required for 'effective action at each step' (Cornish and Clarke, 2008). Roach *et al.* (2005) adopt this crime script approach for analysis of acts of terrorism (or terrorism events). A car bomb attack, for example, is described as comprising of several different scenes ranging from acquiring a vehicle and loading explosives, to getting the vehicle to the target and milking the ensuing 'publicity'. The concept of crime scripts facilitates a mapping of the offender's decision-making at every point, detailing how offenders might identify and respond to crime opportunities. Next, why crime occurs when it does and where it does.

Crime Pattern Theory

Brantingham and Brantingham demonstrate that crime is not randomly distributed in time and space (1984, 2008). The identification and understanding of the clustering is the objective of their Crime Pattern Theory (CPT). In CPT the form of clustering is greatly influenced by factors such as where people live, how they travel about and how 'networks' of people spend time with each other. Individuals,

---

Box 7.1   Routine activities and spatial patterns

Please take a moment to think about how you move around during the course of your average day. We are guessing that you tend to start off from 'home' and then generally proceed by a familiar route either to work, university or the local shops. Then do you perhaps go straight home or to the gym or to a bar? Do you tend to do the same things on the same days of the week? For example, do you take the dog for a walk before you set off for work, or do you play football between 7 and 8 p.m. every Thursday? We are all creatures of habit who like routines and tend to not travel far each day to our places of work and recreation.

Offenders are the same. They spot crime opportunities on their way to the pub the usual time on a Monday, or from the bus they get at 4 p.m. every Friday to visit their dear old mum.

In terms of applying this thinking to crime prevention, if we can work out offenders' routine activities and patterns of movement then we stand more chance of preventing them from realising the opportunities for committing crime which they come across.

---

according to CPT, move around in 'activity spaces' encompassed by several primary 'nodes' such as place of residence, place of work and places of shopping and leisure (e.g. shopping malls, sports centres and pubs), connected by pathways (Brantingham and Brantingham, 1984, 2008). See Box 7.1.

According to CPT, those who commit crime have spatio-temporal movement patterns similar to those that do not commit crime. That is, they move between nodes along pathways. Criminals are therefore likely to commit their initial crimes near learned paths or activity nodes or those of friends, etc., and that is why crime clusters in these areas, some becoming crime generators and some crime attractors. Brantingham and Brantingham advise

> When looking at the representation of crime locations, consider individual offenders and their routine activity spaces; consider networks of friends who engage in some crimes and their joint activity spaces; consider the location of stationary targets and the activity spaces of mobile victims and mobile targets and the catchment areas of fixed targets. The patterns are dynamic. Keeping that in mind will make it possible to understand crime patterns so that crime reduction interventions that produce levels of displacement can be designed.
>
> (2008, p. 91)

Understanding criminal behaviour: linking the individual to environment

Wikström (2005) identifies two central problems of criminological theory which concern identifying causal mechanisms and integrating levels of explanation. The former refers to 'causes and correlates' (e.g. Farrington, 2000) and the latter to the problem of 'connecting individual and ecological levels of explanation' (e.g. Reiss, 1986; Jensen and Akers, 2003, p. 13). In other words criminologists have toiled relentlessly, first to uncover variables which cause individuals to offend and to separate them from those which merely correlate with offending, and second to identify how causes combine to yield criminality.

Criminology teaches us much about relationships between individual characteristics (propensity) and involvement in crime, with developmental (also known as life-course persistent) criminology identifying 'risk factors' associated with future offending (e.g. parental criminality, delinquent peers and truancy – see Farrington, 2002). Of course, being deemed 'at risk', by implication, does not mean that the individual will become criminal, nor that those deemed to be 'not at risk' will not. Human behaviour is not so predictable; the sensible approach accepts that environments and contexts influence whether the individual does or does not offend – this is, as we have seen, the remit of environmental criminology. It would be fair to say that most individual propensity theories fail to elucidate how individual characteristics and propensities are transformed into criminal action or, put another way, what is it about an individual's intersection with a situation/setting that leads them to offend? Wikström claims, '*Motivation* to commit acts of crime arises as an outcome of the *interaction* of individual (crime propensity) and setting (criminogenic features)' (2005, p. 213).

Thus far, a mechanism which links the individual and setting to acts of crime (Wikström, 2005, p. 214) has eluded us. We present the psychological concept of *affordance* as a contender.

Affordance

Please imagine the following:

A man goes hesitantly to see a sex therapist. 'What appears to be the problem, sir?' the therapist asks. 'Well, Doctor, I have come to see you because my wife is convinced that I am preoccupied with sex and that this has become a problem'. The therapist thinks for a moment and then asks if the man will consent to participate in a Rorschach 'ink blot' test to highlight whether there is indeed a problem. He agrees, reluctantly. The therapist asks the man to describe what he sees on each card (i.e. the first thing that enters his head). With each successive card the man answers exactly the same way, 'I see two people, a man and a woman having sex'. The therapist, rather miffed, says, 'Well, sir, you have seen twenty cards now, and with each you have stated that you see a couple having sex. I can only conclude that you are indeed preoccupied with sex. You are perverted, sir!' Unimpressed, the man retorts indignantly, 'I'm a pervert? You're the one with all the dirty pictures!'

The reader is permitted to wonder why we have included what might be loosely termed a joke in a book about evolution and crime. We believe that it provides a light-hearted example of affordance. What the man in the scenario saw in the Rorschach pictures, the therapist did not. What some see as a crime opportunity (e.g. a car with an open window and laptop on the back seat is an opportunity too good to pass up) others do not (e.g. an open window in an unattended car on a hot day is understandable whereas on a cold day it is not).

A more sensible example of affordance is given eloquently by Guillermo Martínez in his novel *The Oxford murders*:

> Indeed, a cat doesn't simply assess a mouse, it assesses it as a prospective meal. But the cat doesn't assess all animals as prospective meals, only mice (2005, p. 53).

For the cat, the mouse affords a prospective meal, since it perceives it as a meal, and not a mouse as such. One presumes the bigger the mouse the bigger the meal it affords. For many humans (and elephants if the popular childhood myth is to be believed) a mouse and its larger rat cousins afford something quite different, namely fear (Roach, 2012). Affordance, put simply, is a perception of what actions come to mind in a particular setting (Pease, 2006). The cat sees the mouse as a prospective meal, while other species see it as something to run away from. This section is about how some settings and environments might afford crime opportunities for some individuals but not others.

Affordance, therefore, is best thought of as the psychology of what actions come to mind in a certain setting. Pease (2006) suggests that 'affordance' is preferable to 'opportunity' because an opportunity implicitly exists outside people. For example, we all have a chance of winning the National Lottery (providing we buy a ticket), whereas affordance is a perception of what actions come to mind in a particular setting and a concept well known to designers. The psychologist and designer Don Norman (1998) gives the example of door handles by way of illustration. A plate on a door affords pushing whereas a handle affords pulling. Norman refers to affordance as the beginning of a psychology of materials implicit in offender decision-making. Pease considers that with regard to criminal behaviour this

> invites consideration of whether and how propensity translates into the proliferation of criminal affordances: whether porcelain figures behind a net curtain on a window ledge are seen as something quaintly old fashioned, or a clue to a probably elderly house holder vulnerable to confrontational burglary; whether the sight of a mobile phone at someone's ear is a pleasant reminder that he or she has friends, or constitutes an invitation to robbery. In short does propensity translate to crime via the perception of affordances?
>
> (2006, p. 58)

In a dedicated criminological study of affordance, Jeanette Garwood (2010) asked a sample of students about their criminality, before administering a Uses of Objects test (see e.g. Getzels and Jackson, 1962; Hudson, 1966). In this test the same sample were shown everyday objects and asked to come up with their possible uses, some of which were criminal. An association was found between an individual's self-reported criminality and the percentage of crime uses they identified. Affordance, it appears, makes a tool a tool, and a tool is not a tool if it is not perceived as such. One will only write on a wall, for example, if one has seen writing on a wall previously; otherwise a wall remains simply a vertical surface for propping up buildings and so on.

Affordances, therefore, vary from person to person and must be acquired and refined by personal or vicarious experience (Pease, 2006). The 'broken windows' hypothesis is founded on the notion that a rundown damaged building (or area) will afford damage in a way that an undamaged one does not (Kelling and Coles, 1997). Similarly, the social psychologist Philip Zimbardo found in an experiment that the perception of a vehicle with a missing wheel afforded vandalism and theft opportunities that a complete vehicle did not (1973, 2007). Taylor and Meenaghan (2006) in their study of decision-making in burglars found that the more experienced were faster at processing cognitively relevant stimuli and cues available from settings, etc., when searching for targets, suggesting expertise. These examples led Pease to suggest 'affordance is, one may speculate, the psychology which links predisposition to setting' (2006, p. 59).

Affordance may well be the psychological link between predisposition and setting but like most other explanations for crime, it focuses on the proximal and the recent but not on the distal. We now turn explicitly to how distal factors might influence criminal behaviour, for example whether we have evolved responses to certain settings which come into play. As evolutionary psychology uses an adaptationist approach to explore cognitive foundations of behaviour (Shackelford and Duntley, 2008), it is best placed to answer such a question. Evolutionary psychologists have tried to explain why certain settings and environments have such profound effects on us. This is known as *environmental aesthetics*, and is a prudent place to begin our exploration of 'hardwired' distal factors which might come into play and influence more proximal factors involved with criminal behaviour.

Distal factors and the ultimate causes of criminal behaviour

> Evolutionary approaches to aesthetics are based on the postulate that emotional responses, because they are such powerful motivators of human behaviour, could not have evolved unless the behaviour they evoked contributed positively, on average, to survival and reproductive success. This is why sugar is sweet and sexual activity is fun.
>
> (Orians and Heerwagen, 1992, p. 555)

Feelings of like and dislike are powerful controls on our behaviour; for example, whether we like someone (or not) strongly influences how we behave towards them. When we dislike someone our behaviour can range from out-and-out hostility through ambivalence to total disregard – possibly passing deception on the way (i.e. feigning liking them). Evolutionary psychologists are of the view that feelings of liking and disliking evolved because they held an adaptive function for our ancestors. To elaborate a little on the example in the quotation above, we enjoy sweet foods because they were the way our ancestors identified nutritious safe foods. Today a sweet tooth, and perhaps giving into such abundant temptation, can be seen as more maladaptive than adaptive (e.g. increasing diabetes and obesity). Some evolutionary psychologists (e.g. Kaplan and Kaplan, 1982; Orians and Heerwagen, 1992) claim that our preference (or dislike) for certain landscapes is explainable in evolutionary terms. So why might this be important to understanding the interaction between criminal behaviour and modern environments?

Environmental aesthetics

Orians and Heerwagen (1992) claim that environmental aesthetics, the study of human responses to landscapes, is a profitable arena in which to study the evolution of aesthetic tastes, because selecting places to live is a universal animal activity that has already been empirically studied and can easily be orientated towards humans. This is because choice of habitat exerts a powerful influence on survival; good habitats should evoke strong positive emotional responses (e.g. higher survival rates prompt people to stay put), poor habitats should evoke weaker or negative ones (e.g. habitat rejection means exploration and resettlement) (Orians and Heerwagen, 1992).The habitats occupied by our ancestors rarely provided the right resources reliably enough to make staying a permanent option. For example, our hunter-gatherer ancestors frequently moved through the landscape, looking for suitable habitats and leading a rather nomadic existence (Campbell, 1985).

Orians suggests that a biological argument that underlies the 'habitat-specific' hypothesis is that natural selection would have favoured those who were motivated to explore and then settle in environments most conducive to their needs, avoiding those not so (for example, those environments with little prospect of regular food and inhabited by predatory animals also looking for a square meal). As we have discussed, evolutionists maintain that it was the different environment of the African savannah with its grassy areas, occasional trees and bushes, and ideally a glint of water, which attracted our ape ancestors down from the trees and shaped the change of evolutionary events which led to modern day humans (*Homo sapiens*). Why did our ape ancestors decide literally to 'up sticks' and take their chances in a newer and more hostile environment for which they were relatively ill-equipped? Simply because it had major advantages over the familiar forest environment. As Smith and Stevens succinctly put it,

> The grassland attracts large animals, which can be hunted for food. Bushes and trees yield accessible fruits. The open views mean dangerous intruders can be easily spotted, and the trees offer both shade and a safe resting place from predators.

> (2002, p. 146)

If habitat preferences co-evolved with the 'intrinsic quality of habitats' (i.e. their survival advantages) then landscape preferences should still be prevalent in modern day humans (Orians and Heerwagen, 1992). After all, if you think about it, the needs of our ancestors were the same as our needs now, namely food, water, shelter, sex and protection from danger. Although fortunately we are nowhere near as likely to be eaten by predators, we are in more danger from hostile conspecifics than our early ancestors were. Although we now seek to obtain the same ultimate needs (survival and sexual reproduction) we do so in environments totally different from those in which our species evolved (discussed in previous chapters). As the amount of evolutionary time that we have lived in urban, mechanised environments is extremely small, it is reasonable to expect that some response patterns which evolved then, in quite different circumstances, can be identified as having influence on our decisions now, even if they are unconscious. So is their evidence for evolved responses to environments valid and if so how does this interact with crime? First, a little reader participation. Please see Box 7.2.

Research on landscape preferences provides evidence that savannah-like environments are better liked by people than other environments (e.g. Falk and Balling, 2010; Orians and Heerwagen, 1992). Tests of preference have generally relied on ratings of photographs or slides of landscapes, but other presentational formats have had the same result, an important point being that most participants had never experienced a savannah-like environment, suggesting that preference is indeed innate. Falk and Balling (2010) suggest that if this innate human preference for savannah-like environments arises from our long evolutionary history then it would be more likely to reveal itself in children than in adults, because adults are likely to have more experience of living in other environments. They found it to be the eight-year-olds in their study who said they would prefer to visit and live in a savannah rather than other proposed environments, though this was an environment that none of them reported ever having experienced.

Box 7.2   Think for a minute about paradise

First, please try and think of a favourite holiday destination you have been to. Where was it? What was the scenery like?

Second, try to think where you would like to live when you retire. Why have you chosen this? What is the attraction?

Third, analyse your answers to the first two questions in evolutionary terms. Is the scenery 'savannah like'? Are these places of beauty, abundant resources and safety?

Was your choice a conscious one? Do you think that your answers show aesthetic 'hardwiring'?

Orians and Heerwagen (1992) continued this line of enquiry in canvassing advice from a plethora of gardeners, photographers and painters about which landscapes their customers considered beautiful. They found that across cultures, people seemed to like semi-open space, slightly hilly, with water, large trees and horizontal views, and with paths trailing into the distance. In sum, a landscape which offers beauty whilst also affording the beauty of not being seen (i.e. places to hide). Kaplan and Kaplan (1982) found additionally that people like environments that they consider easy to read but with a hint of mystery, such as meandering streams and foliage which partially obscures some of the view. They contend that this is not the paradox it first appears, as humans like to think that there are areas with interesting resources yet to be discovered, again consistent with our hunter-gatherer ancestry.

It does appear, therefore, that our preference for landscapes provides strong evidence for the existence of specific hardwiring in the brain for specific environments, but what has this got to do with understanding crime and criminal behaviour?

Ancestral landscapes, environments and crime

Orians and Heerwagen (1992) suggest that a spatial frame of reference (alongside a temporal frame not discussed here) is useful in approaching evolved responses to landscapes. The spatial frame concerns 'the stages of exploration of an unfamiliar landscape, or "habitat", as it is usually referred to in biological literature' (1992, p. 562).

Table 7.1 represents a potted version of Orians and Heerwagen's three stages of exploration of an unfamiliar landscape for habitat selection. As you read the stages of the habitat selection process our ancestors engaged in, you should see the parallel between how our ancestors foraged for food and how a burglar might search for suitable targets. If so, then we believe that our burglar is utilising the evolved process for habitat selection for crime (unconsciously of course).

Table 7.1 Stages of habitat selection

	Exploration of unfamiliar landscape
Stage 1	The decision made on an initial encounter with a new environment is whether to explore it further or avoid it. If to explore move to stage 2.
Stage 2	Information gathering. The individual may draw upon memories and associations between other environments and the resources they provided. Evolved responses are likely to be important at this stage to encourage exploration and to increase the likelihood that attention is given to the most relevant aspects of the habitat. If suitable go to stage 3.
Stage 3	The decision to stay in the environment and to carry out a certain set of activities there, may only relate to a short time or permanent for all behaviours for the whole of the individual's life. If a short period then return to stage 1 and process begins again.

(Orians and Heerwagen, 1992, p. 562)

Prospect-refuge theory (Appleton, 1990) predicts that people should prefer places that allow opportunities to see without being seen, for example places with multiple vantage points and multiple avenues of escape – surveillance and escape were early ancestral strategies for survival and are still so today. As noted earlier, an air of mystery has also proven a popular habitat feature, whether manifested by a winding road or a small bank of trees. Whyte (1980) in a study of urban environments found that popular, small urban areas were likely to contain all these features (suggesting perhaps that evolved preferences are for those that can afford them). With regard to many modern urban settings, the preferred mystery element (that which cannot be seen) should be considered dangerous, fostering apprehension and anxiety instead of intrigue (Orians and Heerwagen, 1992). In his classic New York studies, for example, Oscar Newman found that residents avoided places where they did not have good surveillance (Newman, 1972), presumably because they did not feel safe. Crime rates and vandalism have consistently been found to be higher in places where surveillance is poor (e.g. poor lighting and hidden alleyways). Stoks (1983) found a strong relationship between rape and the physical environment for the same reasons.

Sidebottom and Tilley (2008) posit that 'fear of crime' is felt most acutely by older people residing in areas that they perceive to be high in crime, because evolution has hardwired the most vulnerable to be most on their guard against predators and physically stronger conspecifics. Watch any wildlife programme and you will see that it is the very young, infirm or old gazelle which the lion or cheetah marks out for an easier kill. When the predator fails it is usually because its quarry was on its guard. We pose the question whether trying to reduce fear of crime in the elderly is actually working against (not with) survival mechanisms hardwired by human evolution. One of us had a grandmother who lived in north London and who insisted on having five mortise locks on her front door to keep the criminals at bay, despite her clever-clogs grandson pointing out that statistically she was less likely to become a victim of crime than he was. Although fear of crime kept her in her house after 6 p.m., it could be argued that it kept her safe.

Let us take stock of our exploration of environments and crime so far. Environmental criminology quite comprehensively explains how settings, contexts and situations affect crime opportunities and commission. It does bother itself slightly with the question of how individuals come across crime opportunities and how they might decide to take them. It does not bother itself with how an individual perceives a setting as a crime opportunity in the first place, dismissing this as propensity for crime or inclination. We have also seen how evolutionary psychologists have demonstrated how evolutionary adaptiveness has hardwired the human brain and mind to identify settings and environments and to behave in certain ways, but is there any neurological evidence?

So far we hope that we have demonstrated the influence of ancestral as well as immediate environments on human behaviour. To borrow Stephen Pinker's phrase, we are not all 'blank-slates' to be written on by the environments which we inhabit. Environmental effects may represent the 'software' but we enter this world with a certain amount of 'hardware' engineered by evolutionary forces. As Anthony Walsh and Kevin Beaver put it,

> The evolutionarily primitive parts of the brain (the brain stem) come 'hardwired' at birth, but the development of the higher brain areas (the cerebral cortex) depends to a great extent on environmental 'software' downloaded after birth in response to experience.
>
> (Walsh and Beaver, 2009, p. 20)

The Nobel Prize-winning neuroscientist, Gerald Edelman (1992) distinguishes between distinct brain developmental processes: *experience expected* and *experience dependent.* We suggest both are crucial to our understanding of the linkage between ultimate, distal and proximal influences on behaviour, including risk-taking, anti-social behaviour and crime.

Experience expected developmental processes represent ubiquitous hardwired mechanisms, such as protecting kin, theory of mind and empathy. Edelman suggests that these mechanisms 'expect' exposure to certain environments and experiences as a product of our ancestors' evolutionary experiences, and have developed neural wiring to cope with them. The organism is thereby furnished with built-in coping mechanisms (Walsh and Beaver, 2009). Other coping mechanisms are shaped by exposure to environmental cues. These are thus dependent on the different kinds of environment that an individual experiences, such as different social and cultural environments (Walsh and Beaver, 2009). This may seem like a pompous way of distinguishing instinct and learned behaviour, but it is more than that. Almost every human is capable of acquiring language skills. This capacity is *experience expected* in the sense that communication facilitates cooperation and, as stressed many times in this book, cooperation was and remains necessary for good human functioning in groups. However, the particular language we learn from our parents is *experience dependent.* We all have big brains because big brains help solve problems (so the possession of a big brain is *experience expected*) but the kinds of problem on which the brains are set to work vary hugely across human settlements, so are *experience dependent.* The complexity of these links will become clearer with our discussion of epigenetic mechanisms later in the book.

Here rests our defence against those who would equate evolution-based explanations with biological determinism. Evolution has equipped us with both hardwiring to deal with anticipated and common environments and a capacity to deal with unanticipated and unexpected experiences and environments. The latter is probably what our philosopher friends refer to as 'free will' – the antithesis of determinism (biological or otherwise).

Completing the circle: bringing together the proximal and distal causes of crime (or living fast and dying young)

In an earlier chapter we discussed the universal finding that it is young males who account for most of the crime in any country you care to name, giving shape to one of criminology's most robust findings: the 'age–crime curve' (Gottfredson and Hirschi, 1990, 2003). We looked at how taking an evolutionary perspective can best explain why it is that young males are more inclined to take risks and seek thrills (behaviours inextricably linked with crime and disorder) in rivalry with other males in the competition that is sexual selection.

We have also suggested that traditional criminology struggles with suitable explanations for why it is the world over that young males commit the overwhelming majority of crime. For example, one common line of explanation is that young people who commit criminal offences are more 'present-orientated' than those who do not. In this sense, explaining 'juvenile delinquency' is reducible to a combination of high levels of impulsivity and low levels of self-control (e.g. Gottfredson and Hirschi, 1990, 2003). But, as Margo Wilson and Martin Daly point out, many studies of this nature have little empirical basis 'other than the actions that have defined these youth as offenders' (2006, p. 98). A thoughtful analysis of risk-taking from a Darwinian perspective (M. Wilson *et al.*, 2002) suggests a heady mix of motivational and information-processing factors. Impulsivity is a strong predictor of delinquency and these factors, though beyond our scope here, are important.

In sum, the evidence for general explanations of offending, such as these, comes up rather short. For example, in a study utilising a decision-task with actual monetary consequences, Wilson and Daly (2006) found no significant differences between young offenders and a control group of high school students with regard to discounting the future. This was true even though the young offenders scored higher on a sensation-seeking personality scale, were less likely to have lived with their fathers and had changed schools more often. This supports our premise that behaviour which discounts the future in favour of the present (e.g. using a car without a proper driving licence) does not mean that criminal behaviour is always found along with impulsivity and thrill-seeking per se, since clearly not all young people who are impulsive and thrill-seeking commit crime. So there must be more to it.

From an evolutionary perspective, age-specific risk rates should reflect different evaluations of short-term and long-term rewards, with risk-taking behaviour in general being a function of age. The age–crime curve is indicative of this with most crime being committed by 18–24-year-old males (Farrington, 1986). Wilson and Daly (1985) suggest that this male age group is more likely to be more risk-accepting, engaging in crime and anti-social behaviour, because of the inter-male competition, based on status and material resources, for female mates. And young males, of course, don't just compete with each other but often with higher status and better resourced older males too. This is not 'rocket science' and, as Hill and Chow (2002) suggest, risk-taking might appear to many young males to be the only possible way of obtaining a favourable outcome in their efforts to attract girls, with the associated reproductive opportunities that might ensue.

Conversely, it should follow that older males will be likely to discount the future less than their younger more risk-accepting counterparts. This is also supported by the age–crime curve, with considerations such as gaining status, obtaining regular employment, securing a long-term mate and becoming a parent commonly identified as influential factors which have a 'desistance' effect on risky behaviour including crime. Presumably inter-male rivalry is perceived as being less fierce when you have managed to obtain a long-term mate and have offspring, and mating effort can be shifted to parental investment, facilitating a decrease in a need to engage in risky behaviour (Hill and Chow, 2002). Our primary focus in this chapter, however, is on those who commit most crime and whose behaviour is most anti-social, not with those who have for one reason or another desisted (we save this for the last chapter). For our young males, the sexual competition and the nudge to select the option of risky behaviour go on.

Middle-class children in sixth-form colleges would probably, if pressed, see themselves as having a decent career and living to a ripe old age. In ghettos expectations are very different. Is crime a more tempting option for those who perceive their future prospects to be poor and expect their life to be short?

Let us deal first with the obvious question. If a major influence on whether individuals are more likely to engage in risk-taking behaviour is a perceived short life expectancy, then why is it the young and not the elderly who take the most risks, like driving fast and riding skateboards, or committing shop-theft or burglary? Daly and Wilson (2005) suggest several reasons why the old are generally risk- and crime-averse. First, old age is a relatively new concept – being old is 'evolutionarily novel' – and second:

> The issue is not whether selection has had a chance to act on particular age classes, but whether it has had a chance to act on facultative responsiveness to cues of diminished prowess and low residual reproductive value. Should we not expect males who are confronted with signs of declining competitive ability to become more reckless in the pursuit of one last fertilization?
>
> (2005, p. 56)

Although one of the writers is reminded of a commonly perceived link between middle-aged men and sports cars, he feels obliged to keep it to himself out of respect for his co-writer. Woyciechowski and Kozlowski (1998, cited in Daly and Wilson, 2005) offer more sensible evidence: that worker bees tend to embark on more dangerous foraging missions, both as their wings begin to wear and in response to experimentally induced infections. That is, they take more risks in response to the state of their wings and their health, not necessarily because they are getting old. Either way, they appear to have a sense of their own ephemerality.

Sandeep Mishra and Martin Lalumière suggest that organisms (including humans) base decisions about when to reproduce on environmental cues.

> If the mortality rate due to extrinsic factors (e.g. predation, accidents) is high, it makes little sense for an organism to delay reproduction given the potentially severe costs of not reproducing at all in a dangerous environment. Consequently, effort and energy in this particular environment should be

allocated toward earlier reproduction, minimizing the chances of death without reproducing.

(2008, p. 142)

In an evolutionary context, it is those organisms which most accurately assess their environments (extrinsic factors) and their 'internal mortality' (e.g. healthiness) that are most likely to reproduce successfully. Those who foresee a short life-span (constituting a relatively small window of reproductive opportunity) are more likely to value immediate rather than more distant rewards or, put another way, the 'here and now' is preferable to the 'what might be' in the future. This is known as 'future discounting'. Living for the moment and worrying about tomorrow when it comes is the mantra of the young, as opposed to the middle-aged male more concerned with parenting than mating effort. So what's the evidence, and how might it link being young and male with high levels of crime and anti-social behaviour?

Philips *et al.* (1993) researched the death rates of a sample of Chinese Americans who believed that certain years of birth were susceptible to specific diseases. For example, they believed that 'fire years' were associated with the heart, and therefore with heart disease. Interestingly, they found that among those who believed in a 'year–disease connection', those who contracted a disease associated with their birth year died earlier than those who contracted a disease not associated with their birth year. The findings held for all major causes of death amongst the Chinese American 'year–disease believers' and could not be explained by cohort effects, marital status or any changes in the behaviour of doctors or patients (Philips *et al.*, 1993). What is most interesting about the findings of the Chinese American study is that it demonstrates how certain beliefs about the future can affect human physiology and behaviour, to a point where they can affect resistance to disease. It is with behaviour, not disease, which we concern ourselves here.

The astute reader will already have anticipated the point we are about to make: that one interpretation of these findings is that humans possess a sensitivity to 'time horizons' (Mishra and Lalumière, 2008). Put simply, we have evolved a kind of inbuilt mortality clock, a psychological mechanism which gives us humans (and other animals) a sense of our own likely life-span. What Philips *et al.* (1993) are suggesting, essentially, is that it is the environment which is key in helping us to predict our own life-span as we pick up (not necessarily consciously) environmental cues (like the beliefs about longevity held by the sample of Chinese Americans) about the probability of future life chances (including reproductive). The question begged here is the extent to which the decision to engage in anti-social and criminal behaviour is influenced by an individual's assessment of their current and future environments and the behavioural options available to them to meet their reproductive needs. For example, do those who experience economic disadvantage or poor health perceive their 'expected outcomes' to be poor? As a consequence, are they more likely to discount time, choosing to take risks (including indulging in criminal behaviour) now, in preference to waiting on an uncertain or predictably poor future? So is this a sound evolutionary based explanation for why it is young males who commit most of the crime? Let's take a brief look at the evidence.

To re-state the pioneering homicide research of Wilson and Daly: they found that many homicides occurred as a direct result of young male-on-male competition over status or mates (1996). Of course both of these, evolutionarily, are inextricably linked. Daly and Wilson examined homicide rates and reproductive timing (e.g. age when one first becomes a parent) as a function of 'economic inequality' (e.g. rich or poor) and 'local life expectancy' (average age of mortality in a given geographical area) and found the homicide rate increased as local life expectancy decreased (even after statistically removing the effects of homicide on life expectancy) (Wilson and Daly, 1996; Daly and Wilson, 2005). This is consistent with an evolutionary based prediction that in terms of life expectancy males would escalate competition, and that increasing rates of violence (including homicide) would reflect this. Indeed, Daly and Wilson (2005) found homicide to be highest in areas with the largest wealth differentiation, where male competition for sexual selection was highest and life expectancy lowest.

It might be true that although homicide rates are highest among those men with the least to lose (the unemployed, unattached, with little prospect of future opportunities), this might be a correlational rather than causal relationship. Those who never marry may not do so because they are anti-social in the first place. Daly and Wilson, pragmatically, acknowledge this:

> It is possible, of course, these demographic statuses have no direct causal relevance to the likelihood that a man will kill or be killed, but are simply correlates of other determinants (2005, p. 59).

Interestingly, however, they offer evidence to counter this in research which they conducted with divorced and widowed men. Here they found that these men revert to the high homicide rates seen among their same-age single male counterparts (Daly and Wilson, 2005), suggesting that being 'currently unmarried' is the real causal determinant of the use of risk-taking and often reckless behaviour as tactics in sexual competition. Once a man is back 'on the market', so to speak, then it appears he is likely to return to his old risk-taking ways in pursuit of a new mate, especially if he lives in an area of economic disadvantage with low levels of life expectancy for the average inhabitant (Wilson and Daly, 1996).

Chapter summary and reprise

To recapitulate, we have looked at how environments can influence behaviour and posited that the concept of affordance explains why some recognise criminal opportunities where most do not. We have introduced and discussed evidence for the existence of psychological hardwiring created through evolution, which enables us to deal with both anticipated and unfamiliar environmental experiences. For example, why it is that young males with least to lose (in terms of 'mate-attracting resources'), residing in areas of highest economic disadvantage and lowest life expectancy, are most likely to 'discount the future' and engage in crime and anti-social behaviour as part of an alternative strategy for success. The dangerous competitive behaviour which ensues as a consequence entails an implicit 'disdain for the future', exacerbated by the sense that one is living in 'the sort of social milieu in which one's future may be cut short' (Daly and Wilson, 2005, p. 59). We reserve suggestions for how youth crime and anti-social behaviour might be reduced for the last chapter.

8   The ultimate mystery
of inheritance

Introduction

Life history theory contends that the scheduling and duration of key events in human life are shaped by natural selection, so as to optimise reproductive success. Accordingly, some of these will vary depending on the ecological niche in which the organism finds itself (Charnov 1993). Life history theory has its origins in r/K selection theory (MacArthur and Wilson 1967).

Two key human decisions concern whether to reproduce now or later, and how much care to devote to each offspring. Life history theory characterises the trade-off between quantity and quality of offspring. Organisms which are said to be 'r selected' have many offspring and nurture them little or not at all. 'K selected' species have fewer offspring and invest more in each one. In unstable or unpredictable environments, r selection predominates, since the ability to reproduce quickly is crucial. In stable or predictable environments, K selection predominates as the ability to compete successfully for limited resources is crucial. Populations of K selected organisms are typically somewhat more steady in numbers, and often close to the maximum that the environment can bear. One can apply r/K selection theory to both inter- and intra-species variation. Life history theory makes interesting predictions about (for example) the relationship between child sexual abuse and menarche, and 'extrinsic risks' like pathogen prevalence, against which parental care is not a defence (see Quinlan, 2007). High extrinsic threats, it is theorised, move people towards r selection (though Quinlan reveals a more complex picture). The future discounting work of Wilson and Daly, which we described earlier, can be thought of in terms of life history theory, with future discounting moving adolescent boys without prospects towards the r end of the r–K continuum.

If you accept that there is ample evidence that the situation you find yourself in determines the timing and duration of key life events, and that the purpose of this is to tailor your life so as to maximise your chances of reproductive success, how is this achieved? One answer to that is epigenetics.

The epigenetics revolution

The heading above is the title of a book by Nessa Carey which is a brilliant introduction to the topic (Carey, 2012). By the time you read this we hope there will be a second edition. We hope you read it, because the importance of the topic, in contexts as diverse as cancer treatment and violence prevention, is immense. Its importance is mirrored by the large number of texts on this subject for the general or student reader (for example Francis 2011; Spector 2012; Allis *et al.*, 2007), the launch of a journal entitled *Epigenetics* in 2007[1] and burgeoning research programmes in many universities. So what is epigenetics? 'Epi' is the Greek prefix indicating 'above' or 'beyond', so epigenetics means 'beyond genetics'. Let us take an example with which you will probably be familiar. You will be aware that at conception, the cells which will become you can develop into any of the fifty-five different cell types which make up an adult human. They are 'totipotent'. As you develop, they lose that capacity. A skin cell cannot turn into a nerve cell even if it is surrounded by other nerve cells. A totipotent cell *can* do this. The reason why this causes excitement among medical scientists is that it offers the possibility of re-growing cells of the right type, for example to repair spinal injuries. Totipotent cells placed at the site of a spinal injury will proliferate *as nerve cells*. The situation is more complex than this, of course, both physiologically and ethically, since the source of totipotent cells is early stage aborted human foetuses. The mystery is why do cells, as they develop, differentiate so that they can't stay totipotent? Their chromosomes have not changed. The genes on those chromosomes have not changed. What has changed? The answer is epigenetics, the regulation of gene expression. There are good elementary accounts of the chemistry by which this occurs (see for example Francis, 2011) and we will not venture into that fascinating area of research here. In brief, and over-simply, the regulation of gene expression (their degree of protein production) lies behind the process. We noted in an earlier chapter that the ENCODE project recently demonstrated how much more complex than hitherto thought was the switching of gene expression by what had until then been regarded as 'junk DNA'.

Before going on to describe a real-life example of epigenetic modification, let us say why it merits a place in a book about evolution and crime. Imagine you live in a cosy ecological niche to which you, as a species, are well adapted. Let's say something unusual happens to the environment (a famine or being over-run by a competing group); there's nothing you can do about it genetically. Your genes have been much as they now are for many generations, and you can't mutate your way out of the problem. That happens far too slowly to be of any use to your developing foetus. What can you do? It would be nice if evolution had equipped you with a sort of emergency toolkit to ensure that the next generation is *slightly* better equipped to deal with the changed world into which they will be born. Perhaps we have such a toolkit.

The hungry winter

This example is found in the Nessa Casey introductory text cited. In September 1944, with World War II coming to a close, the German army was in retreat. Their occupation of the north-west Netherlands was threatened by Allied troops, moving from the south. To aid the Allied advance, the Dutch government in exile ordered a railway strike. The occupying German army retaliated with a food embargo. This coincided with an exceptionally severe winter, and the flooding of fields and blowing up of rail tracks by the retreating German army. All in all, a severe famine was the result. Because of excellent Dutch medical records, some good was retrieved from the dreadful suffering by plotting the consequences of going hungry on the development of babies in the womb during the hungry winter. Those whose mothers were in the early stages of pregnancy at the time were, when they reached adulthood, more obese than those born before or after the famine. Those whose mothers were in the last three months of pregnancy during the famine were born small and stayed relatively small all their lives. Boys who were in the womb during the famine more often exhibited some behavioural problems, including anti-social personality disorder. Those exposed to famine while in the womb suffered more health problems in later life.

Imagine yourself as a foetus trying to work out how best to equip yourself for life in the outside world, and getting information about your mother's nutrition through her bloodstream. If you detected that she was going short of food during the early stages of pregnancy, you might say 'I'll take what I can get now, and set my metabolism up so that I'm not too picky about what I eat. OK, I might end up obese, but things seem tough out there, so that will be the least of my worries'. If, on the other hand, mother was well fed until late pregnancy, you might surmise that things have just got rougher outside, so it would be as well to limit your growth, because 'That way I'm more likely to be born alive, what with us big-brained human babies having heads so big they test the limits of the birth canal. Mum is in a bad way already, and I'll need fewer calories once I'm born, since times are getting harder. You should have been in this womb a few months ago. It was great. All you could ingest'. As for the male-specific increase in anti-social behaviour, foetal thinking might be 'It's turning into a dog-eat-dog world out there. I'd better turn out selfish'. Obviously we are not suggesting that foetuses mutter to themselves in the womb, simply that the epigenetic changes may have yielded just the short-term adjustments that would best fit the new baby to what the 'long range food forecast' of the womb had predicted. Tim Spector makes the same point after a discussion on research using chickens: 'This suggested how epigenetic changes could provide survival advantages. Environmental stresses could prime future generations to be able to cope better in the same situations . . . a brilliantly effective form of short-term evolution' (2012, p. 38).

In recent years, epigenetic effects have popped up all over the place, being seen in the epigenetic effects of the warmth of maternal care (in mice), cancer growth and diet. Much work has been done on the stress response. This is measured by levels of cortisol, a hormone produced by the adrenal glands. Cortisol levels are elevated in adults who had traumatic childhoods. This effect is thought to be epigenetic. As Nessa Carey writes:

> The reason scientists have hypothesised that the adult sequelae of early childhood abuse may have an epigenetic component is that we're dealing with scenarios where a triggering event continues to have consequences long

after the trigger itself has disappeared. . . . Imprinted genes get switched off at certain stages in development, and stay off throughout the rest of life. Indeed, epigenetic modifications are the only known mechanism for maintaining cells in a particular state for exceptionally long periods of time.

(p. 236)

It should be noted that there is some evidence from the 'hungry winter' work that some epigenetic effects extend to the generation beyond that where the child was in the womb. The Cambridge longitudinal study, overseen by Professor David Farrington at Cambridge University, now has data over three generations which, when fully analysed, may well tell us about possible epigenetic effects over three generations in relation to impulsivity and criminality.

It may be that the possible epigenetic effect whereby abuse leads to chronic high stress is counter-reproductive. It may be that there's no selection advantage one way or the other. Or it may be that there is something about the EEA which made stressed behaviours reproductively valuable. There is an obvious link with the work on MAOA expression described earlier. This line of work could be very important indeed. Even as it stands, avoiding childhood abuse will reduce hypertension fifty years down the line. One of the behavioural correlates of stress is reduced exploration and play. Perhaps there is something (but not much) to be said for being stressed in an environment where you are abused. You explore less and hide more.

Getting closer to crime, what else do we know about the possible epigenesis of violence? Nagin and Tremblay (1999) identified four trajectories of human aggression: a chronic problem trajectory, a high-level near desister trajectory, a moderate-level desister trajectory or a no-problem trajectory. They speculated that there may be an epigenetic difference between people passing along the different trajectories. They tested this (necessarily crudely) by looking at methylation levels in two genes deemed relevant to aggression. Methylation is the most studied form of epigenetic change and consists of attaching a methyl 'tag' to a gene which regulates its expression. Methyl is a chemical group containing one carbon atom bonded to three hydrogen atoms. (The journal *Epigenetics* is the official journal of the DNA Methylation Society, to give you some idea of the emphasis placed on methyl tagging as a means of regulating gene expression.)

Why should you be interested?

Well, if you or a loved one plan to get cancer any time soon, there is a good chance that this way of thinking offers hope for better treatments.

The last few years have seen a revolution in our views of cancer. Till lately it was thought that single mutations in a cancer gene usually start the process. This is unlikely. Epigenetics is now understood as the key in the cancer-forming process, by ensuring the survival of the abnormal cancer cells.

(Spector, 2012, p. 197)

But we are not oncologists. We are crime scientists interested in evolution. What's exciting us about this new field is that, as Spector has suggested, it has introduced the concept of a sort of short-run, one-or-two-generation means that evolution has devised of tweaking our genotype to match the out-of-womb conditions which the neonate anticipates it will face. Since our ultra-sociality is the means whereby we maintain stable communities, these tweaks may well be crucial. There are many difficult ethical and other obstacles to doing fundamental epigenetic work on humans, and you will find more research about plant than human epigenesis. The first task is to establish, by the imperfect methods available to us, how epigenesis works in the onset of violent and manipulative behaviour. We must then figure out how that might have contributed to the agenda of natural selection. Is there an evolutionary upside to the epigenetic changes thought to be brought about by child abuse? If there is, surely this is a case where we must work against the grain of what nature has given us. The idea of therapeutic child abuse is wholly repugnant. Let us speculate a little. Let us say that the epigenetic changes which yield high cortisol levels, and therefore high stress, had a survival function during EEA. Let us say that less exploration and play was safer when the people you were likely to meet while playing or exploring were likely to do you harm. Does the hypertension and shortened life that will follow make that worthwhile? Never. And we have shown how much less danger now lurks than during the EEA. If abuse-activated stress was just about worth it in the past to get you to the age at which you could reproduce, surely it is not so now in most parts of the world. Every time we seem to have reached a policy conclusion in this book, it has been in terms of the crucial importance of making the environment, both in the womb and later, in terms of diet and lifestyle, safer and better nourished. That is scarcely the eugenic agenda which many social scientists seem to fear.

9 So what?

Introduction

In this very short chapter, we will seek to persuade you that the Darwinian perspective on crime and other social issues holds promise for policy and practice. The genius Michael Faraday, when asked about the utility of the dynamo he had just invented, is said to have replied 'What use is a baby?' Certainly, to be accepted as a major strand in the study of crime and criminality, Darwinian thinking has to overcome a century during which the discipline of more conventional criminology has struggled to reach its current, still unimpressive position. Criminology should be humble. When one looks at the speed of development of research and theory in many biological sciences and the links that are emerging between disciplines, humility is the only defensible response. Look at the literature of criminology (the average age of research referenced, the citation of books rather than journals) and the absence of hybrid disciplines and research units, and you see the signs of a discipline that needs a shot in the arm. For example University College London has a Centre for Genetics and Anthropology, and such hybrid research groups are being created in many universities. This phenomenon is reflected even in such a crude measure as journal titles, with many newer journals addressing interstitial areas (e.g. *Journal of Nanobiotechnology*), and the proliferation of new journals, many of them offshoots of the original journal *Nature*, reflecting areas in which development is speedy (such as *Nature Photonics*, new in 2007; *Nature Nanotechnology*, new in 2006). Examples outside the *Nature* stable include *Biodata Mining*, new in 2008; *Systems and Synthetic Biology*, new in 2007; *Computational Biology*, new in 2005. In contrast, journals with 'Criminology' in their title seldom get more cross-disciplinary than an indication of their methodological focus (*Journal of Quantitative Criminology*) or their geographic location (*European Journal of Criminology*).

We are proposing a *paradigm shift* in criminology. In 1962, Thomas Kuhn's book *The structure of scientific revolution* (Kuhn, 1962) characterised scientific progress as a 'series of peaceful interludes punctuated by intellectually violent revolutions', and in those revolutions 'one conceptual world view is replaced by another' (p. 10). It's something of a stretch to suggest that Darwinian thinking could yield a paradigm shift in criminology. After all, this is a viewpoint about which a large minority of people (in some nations a majority) remains sceptical, and there is a great deal of inertia to be overcome. But evolutionary thinking in psychology, neuroscience, anthropology and to some extent even economics, is on the rise. Criminology is behind the curve amongst social science disciplines in recognising the significance of evolution in its theorising. In any event, we do not suggest a privileged position for evolutionary thinking, just a wider discipline base on which to build, such as we see in Anthony Walsh and Lee Ellis' criminology textbook (Walsh and Ellis, 2007).

What are the implications of the arguments advanced in this book, particularly in respect of how we organise society rather than how we engage with those who have already embarked upon a criminal career? A more comprehensive list can be referred to elsewhere (Ellis, 2008).

Childcare agencies should monitor step-parents more carefully than biological parents

In engineering and technology, a rough prototype of a new idea is often constructed as a 'proof of concept'. The most obvious proof of concept in this kind of study (let us call it evolutionary criminology) is the Wilson and Daly work on infanticide (Daly and Wilson, 2007). If they are right, the education and monitoring of step-parents would save the lives of many children.

Seek to ensure that adolescents can envisage success in some terms which will enhance their perceived mating opportunities

Daly and Wilson's work on the limited time horizons of disadvantaged adolescent males highlights the importance of persuading them about the feasibility of future achievement so that they do not behave self-destructively by seeking premature reproductive success.

Seek to ensure more gender equality of birth and infant mortality

Pinker's observations on optimal sex ratios (Pinker, 2011), following from the work of Guttentag and Secord (Guttentag and Secord, 1983), ring warning bells about keeping the peace in societies with an excess of males. Anne Campbell's survival hypothesis (Campbell, 1999) invites synthesis with epigenetics.

Resource pre-natal care more generously

The work on epigenetics described earlier makes clear the crucial importance of pre-natal care for adult wellbeing over two, perhaps three, generations. The evolutionary interpretation of epigenetic gene regulation is a game changer for *all* the human sciences.

Research late Pleistocene settlement design and apply lessons to plans for crime reduction

When, in the EEA, our forebears went foraging, they could do so well or poorly. What does good foraging look like? A good forager will bring home a large haul of nutritious stuff, while expending least energy by travelling the shortest possible distance, which is necessary both to conserve energy personally and to avoid venturing into unfamiliar territory where danger lurks from other bands or non-human predators. You can witness the modern forager in 'pick your own' fruit farms, where people exhaust the good fruit on nearby bushes before moving (not far) to more promising areas. Children do this too, but their foraging is often restricted by parental calls to return.

Many offenders operate as optimal foragers. The notion of the optimal forager has been explicitly imported into the criminological vocabulary to explain spatio-temporal patterns, and it fits wonderfully well (Johnson *et al.*, 2009) and seems to apply cross-nationally (Johnson *et al.*, 2007). The ability to predict the location and duration of burglary spates has been used in police resource allocation with some success. The article 'Disrupting the optimal forager' (Fielding and Jones, 2012) encapsulates the thinking. The same 'optimal forager' phenomena have been observed in respect of other crime types, without the label being explicitly applied (Daly and Wilson, 1988; Youstin *et al.*, 2011; Summers *et al.*, 2007). The approach has even been extended to the prediction of insurgent activity in Iraq (Townsley *et al.*, 2008).

The same research group has definitely determined the pattern of burglary according to street configuration (Johnson and Bowers, 2010). This is a strand of research which, combined with awareness of the size of EEA human groups (R. I. M. Dunbar, 1992) and the configuration of EEA settlements (Boehm, 2012) could yield a refinement of specifications for lower crime neighbourhoods.

Facilitate retraining of criminology teachers in evolutionary theory

This is self-evident. Without some basic awareness of evolutionary thinking amongst those who teach criminology in universities and colleges, there will be no long-term progress. We do not underestimate the difficulties and dangers of this task. One of us has been called a racist for daring to teach on evolutionary topics, and even an intro-ductory book as modest as this will be met with hostility. It is profoundly depressing to remember the college teacher quoted in our introductory chapter, who said that she did not teach evolution and she would be in trouble if she did.

We must mention an ambitious initiative targeting a wide range of social problems. This is D. S. Wilson's Evolution Institute.[1] Below are listed the Institute's 'focal topics' and the first sentence (or two) of the website description of each. Some, perhaps all, of these are relevant to crime. It would be a pity if criminologists were absent from its workshops and activities.

1   *Education* Early childhood education is an example of a system that isn't working, despite everyone's best intentions. Some of the foremost authorities

on child development and education are already stressing the need for an evolutionary perspective. The Evolution Institute brought them together in a workshop held at the University of Miami on November 14–16, 2008.

2 *Ethics after Darwin* Ethical inquiry requires assumptions about human nature. In the past, these assumptions have been based on intuition or scientific knowledge available at the time. Today, we are witnessing an explosion of knowledge about the nature of our species from an evolutionary perspective.

3 *Evolutionary mismatch and what to do about it* Finding the right interventions is important because restoring the ancestral environment is not always the most feasible or desirable option. Natural selection adapts organisms to their past environments and has no ability to foresee the future. When the environment changes, adaptations to past environments can misfire in the current environment.

4 *Evonomics [sic]* Current economic theory is dominated by a mathematical tradition initially inspired by 19th century physics, whose assumptions are so constraining that *Homo economicus* bears almost no relation to *Homo sapiens*. Policies that are derived from such a false view of human nature are highly likely to fail.

5 *Failed states and nation building* The rise of a centralised state that commands real authority throughout its territory can be seen as the reverse of the process by which a state loses its authority and gradually crumbles into a 'failed state.' A key aspect of state building involves establishing the internal bonds that make it possible for a disparate congery of smaller-scale groups to unite within a larger framework. Both formation of larger social units from smaller ones and its reverse, disintegration, have been studied intensively from the perspective of cultural and social evolution.

6 *Play* Our goal is to develop a blueprint for restoring neighbourhoods as cooperative units and ideal environments for child development. A hidden problem of modern life is the lack of opportunity for self-directed outdoor play in children.

7 *Quality of Life from an Evolutionary Perspective* Evolution is supposed to adapt organisms to their environments, but the human species seems bent upon its own destruction. Everyone is familiar with the drumbeat of potential calamities: violent conflict ... weapons of mass destruction ... overpopulation ... economic collapse ... extreme inequality ... environmental degradation. ... We expect ... a new agenda for basic scientific research, policy formulation, and policy implementation.

8 *Risky Adolescent Behaviour* High-risk activities in adolescence—unprotected sex, substance abuse, violence, and other forms of risky behaviour—remain a pervasive and costly problem in Western societies, despite extensive efforts to prevent or reduce these activities through intervention programmes. An evolutionary perspective provides a fresh alternative to the mental health model.

9 *Rules as Genotypes in Cultural Evolution* Cultural evolution has long been loosely compared to genetic evolution, but only recently has this comparison

been taken seriously. In books such as *Evolution in Four Dimensions* (Jablonka and Lamb, 2006), learning and symbolic thought are treated as mechanisms of cross-generational inheritance that function in the same way as genetic inheritance mechanisms.

In an article in *New Scientist* magazine in 2011, Wilson gave a practical example of his work stimulating people to design and operate a neighbourhood park. He describes the background theory as follows:

> groups of people are capable of managing common resources when certain conditions are met. The conditions, in a nutshell, are that the group and its purpose must be clearly defined; costs and benefits must be equally shared; decision-making must be by consensus; misconduct should be monitored; sanctions should start out mild and escalate only as needed; conflict resolution should be fast and fair; the group must have the authority to manage its affairs; and the relationship of the group with others must be appropriately structured.[2]

Finally . . .

In short, evolutionary criminology is not even the baby about whose usefulness Faraday queried his critics. It is a recently fertilised ovum immersed in uncongenial amniotic fluid and with a father (traditional criminology) set upon termination of the pregnancy. That is enough hyperbole, although it is perhaps worth noting that the social policy prescriptions emerging tentatively from Darwinian thinking would be more congenial to liberal democracies than regimes of the right.

We have a last request to the reader. Think about this. Read about it. Reach your own decisions. Don't be discouraged by the eye-popping hostility of those who say you shouldn't.

Notes

1 Crime and evolution: strange companions?

1 http://law2.umkc.edu/faculty/projects/ftrials/scopes/scopes2.htm (accessed 30 June 2012).
2 http://www.goodreads.com/author/quotes/219349.DanielPatrickMoynihan (accessed 22 November 2012).
3 http://www.nap.edu/openbook.php?record_id=6024&page=24 (accessed 28 June 2012).
4 http://news.bbc.co.uk/1/hi/sci/tech/4648598.stm (accessed 28 June 2012).
5 http://www.gallup.com/poll/114544/darwin-birthday-believe-evolution.aspx (accessed 28 June 2012).

2 People who need people?

1 http://www.nature.com/encode/ (accessed 10 September 2012).
2 Any local population of individuals of the same species is known as an avatar, causing confusion for players of computer games.
3 A clade is a group with a common species origin.
4 There are exceptions, where people deliberately ingest parasites to combat auto-immune diseases. An account is given in *New Scientist*, 3 August 2011, pp. 6–7.
5 http://www.darwinawards.com/darwin/darwin1996–07.html (accessed 3 October 2012).
6 It's much more complex than this, insofar as his death forgoes further paternal protection of the children.
7 The tragedy of the commons is the depletion of a shared resource by individuals, acting independently and rationally according to each one's self-interest, despite their understanding that depleting the common resource is contrary to their long-term best interests. An example is the current depletion of fish stocks.

3 Theory of mind, empathy and criminal behaviour

1 http://www.bbc.co.uk/news/uk-england-leeds-15870279 (accessed 27 September 2012). For the full news report.
2 http://www.youtube.com/watch?v=rZTAW0vPE1o (accessed 22 September 2012).
3 http://healing.about.com/cs/empathic/a/uc_empathtraits.htm (accessed 27 August 2012).
4 http://www.psi-zone.net/aboutme/empath.htm (accessed 27 August 2012).
5 http://www.commonlaw.com/Hammurabi.html (accessed 3 October 2012).

6 We do not feel it necessary to list all ten areas here but helpfully direct the reader to Simon Baron-Cohen's book *Zero Degrees of Empathy*, London: Allen Lane, pp. 19–28 for a fuller discussion.

4 The sense of fairness and the emergence of criminal justice

1 http://www.biblehistory.net/newsletter/scapegoat.htm (accessed 25 September 2012).
2 The first author recalls one of his grandparents saying something to the same effect but was insulated from any guilt on the grounds that he wasn't listening properly.
3 http://obscenedesserts.blogspot.co.uk/2006/08/ep-thompson-uncommon.html (accessed 25 September 2012).
4 http://news.bbc.co.uk/1/hi/world/africa/2115644.stm (accessed 25 September 2012).
5 http://www.achievement.org/autodoc/page/par0bio-1 (accessed (appropriately) on 4 July 2012).
6 http://www.guardian.co.uk/uk/2007/jan/13/secondworldwar.world (accessed 25 September 2012).

5 Violence

1 As tragically happened on 20th July 2012, in Aurora, Colorado. The attack happened during the screening of a new Batman film, *The dark knight rises*. Twelve people were killed and fifty-nine wounded allegedly by gunman James Holmes, a 24-year-old Ph.D. student. See http://www.bbc.co.uk/news/world-us-canada-18921492 (accessed 1 August 2012).
2 http://www.viking.ucla.edu/hrolf/berserkers.html (accessed 28 September 2012).
3 Or the mother's young with other sexual partners. It has been noted that babies are more often said to resemble their fathers than their mothers, an alleged evolutionary device to keep the duped male in the home.
4 This is not in any sense a criticism of Pinker, who cites Gurr and is thoroughly scrupulous in acknowledging the work of others. It just seems a pity that Gurr was not equally fêted.

6 Crime: it's a man thing?

1 http://www.hhmi.org/biointeractive/gender/Y_evolution.html (accessed 6 October 2012).
2 http://unstats.un.org/unsd/demographic/sconcerns/mortality/mort2.htm (accessed 22 September 2012).
3 Campbell, personal communication, 2012.

8 The ultimate mystery of inheritance

1 http://www.landesbioscience.com/journals/epigenetics/archive/ (accessed 22 January 2013).

9 So what?

1 http://evolution-institute.org/ (accessed 1 October 2012).
2 http://www.newscientist.com/article/mg21128270.300-evolutionary-theory-can-make-street-life-better.html (accessed 6 October 2012).

References

Allis, C. D., Jenuwein, T., and Reinberg, D. (2007). *Epigenetics*. New York: Cold Spring Harbor Laboratory Press.

Amodio, D., and Frith, C. (2006). Meeting of minds: the medial frontal cortex and social cognition. *Nature Reviews Neuroscience*, 7, 268–77.

Appleton, J. (1990). *The Symbolism of Habitat*. Seattle, Washington: University of Washington Press.

Athens, L. (1989). *The creation of dangerous violent criminals*. London: Routledge.

Avis, J., and Harris, P. (1991). Belief-desire reasoning among Baka children: evidence for a universal conception of mind. *Child Development*, 62 (3), 460–7.

Ayres, M., and Murray, L. (2005). *Arrests for recorded crime (notifiable offences) and the operation of certain police powers under PACE, England and Wales 2004/05. Home Office Statistics Bulletin*. London: Home Office.

Barash, D. P. (2012). *Homo mysterious: evolutionary puzzles of human nature*. Oxford: Oxford University Press.

Baron-Cohen, S. (2011). *Zero degrees of empathy: a new theory of human cruelty*. London: Allen Lane.

Barrett, L., Dunbar, R., and Lycett, J. (2002). *Human evolutionary psychology*. Basingstoke: Palgrave.

Batson, C. (2009). These things called empathy: eight related but distinct phenomena. In (eds.) J. Decety and W. Ickes. *The social neuroscience of empathy*, Cambridge, MA: MIT Press.

Beck, E., and Tolnay, S. (1990). The killing fields of the Deep South: the market for cotton and the lynching of blacks 1882–1930. *American Sociological Review*, 55 (4), 526–39.

Berkman, M. B., Pacheco, J. S., and Plutzer, E. (2008). Evolution and creationism in America's classrooms: a national portrait. *PLoS Biology*, 6 (5).

Berkowitz, L. (1989). Frustration-aggression hypothesis: Examination and reformulation. *Psychological Bulletin*, 106(1), 59–73.

Blackburn, R. (1993). *The psychology of criminal conduct: theory, research and practice*. Chichester: Wiley.

Blake, E., and Gannon, T. (2008). Social perception deficits, cognitive distortions, and empathy deficits in sex offenders: a brief review. *Trauma, Violence, and Abuse*, 9 (1), 34–55.

Boehm, C. (2012). *Moral origins: the evolution of virtue, altruism, and shame*. New York: Basic Books.

Book, A., and Quinsey, V. (2004). Psychopaths: cheaters or warrior-hawks? *Personality and Individual Differences*, 36 (1), 33–45.

Brantingham, P.J., and Brantingham, P.L. (1984) *Patterns in Crime*. New York: Macmillan.

Brantingham, P.J., and Brantingham, P.L. (1993). Environment, routine and situation. Toward a pattern theory of crime. In Clarke, R.V. and Felson, M. (Eds), *Routine Activity and Rational Choice*. New Brunswick, NJ: Transaction Publishers.

Brantingham, P.J., and Brantingham, P.L. (2008) Crime Pattern Theory. In Wortley, R. and Mazerolle, L. (Eds.) *Environmental Criminology and Crime Analysis*. Cullompton, Devon: Willan. 78–93.

Burke, D. (2001). Empathy in sexually offending and nonoffending in adolescent males. *Journal of Interpersonal Violence*, 16 (3), 222–33.

Burke, R. H. (2005). *An introduction to criminological theory*. Cullompton, Devon: Willan.

Buss, D. (2004). *Evolutionary psychology: the new science of the mind*, 2nd edn. Boston, MA: Pearson.

Buss, D. (2005). *The murderer next door: why the mind is designed to kill*. New York: Penguin.

Buss, D., and Hawley, P. (2011). *The evolution of personality and individual differences*. Oxford: Oxford University Press.

Buss, D. M. (1994) *The evolution of desire: Strategies of human mating*. New York: Basic Books.

Buss, D. M., and Shackelford, T.K. (1997). Human aggression in evolutionary psychological perspective. *Clinical Psychology Review*, 17 (6), 605–19.

Campbell, A. (1999). Staying alive: evolution, culture, and women's intrasexual aggression. *Behavioural and Brain Sciences*, 22 (2), 203–14.

Campbell, A. (2012). *A mind of her own: the evolutionary psychology of women*, 2nd edn. Oxford: Oxford University Press.

Campbell, B. (1985). *Human Evolution, third edition*. New York: Aldine.

Cantor, J.M., Blanchard, R., Paterson, A.D.M.B., and Bogaert, A.F. (2002). How Many Gay Men Owe Their Sexual Orientation to Fraternal Birth Order? *Archives of Sexual Behavior,* 31(1), 63–71.

Caprara, G., Cinanni, V., D'Imperio, G., Passerini, S., Renzi, P., and Travaglia, G. (1985). Indicators of impulsive aggression: present status of research on irritability and emotional susceptibility scales. *Personality and Individual Differences*, 6 (6), 665–74.

Caprara, G., Barbaranelli, C., and Zimbardo, P. (1996). Understanding the complexity of human aggression: affective, cognitive, and social dimensions of individual differences in propensity toward aggression. *European Journal of Personality*, 10 (2), 133–55.

Carey N. (2012). *The epigenetics revolution: how modern biology is rewriting our understanding of genetics, disease and inheritance*. London: Icon.

Carver, C., Johnson, S., Joormann, J., Kim, Y., and Nam, J. (2011). Serotonin transporter polymorphism interacts with childhood adversity to predict aspects of impulsivity. *Psychological Science*, 22 (5), 589–95.

Cashdan, E. (1993). Attracting mates: effects of paternal investment on mate attraction strategies. *Ethology and Sociobiology*, 14 (1), 1–23.

Caspi, A., McClay, J., Moffitt, T., Mill, J., Martin, J., Craig, I., Taylor, A., and Poulton, R. (2002). Role of genotype in the cycle of violence in maltreated children. *Science*, 297 (5582), 851–4.

Charnov, E. (1993). *Life history invariants: some explorations of symmetry in evolutionary ecology*. Oxford: Oxford University Press.

Christie, N. (1977). Conflicts as Property. *British Journal of Criminology*, 17 (1), 1–15.

Clarke, R.V., and Eck, J. (2003) *Become a Problem-Solving Analyst*. Cullompton, Devon, Willan.

Clarke, R.V., and Felson, M. (1993). *Introduction: Criminology, routine activity, and rational choice. Advances in Criminological Theory, Vol. 5.* New Brunswick, NJ: Transaction Publishers.

Cohen, L.E., and Felson, M. (1979) Social-change and crime rate trends – Routine activity approach. *American Sociological Review*, 44(4), 588–608.

Cohen, T., Panter, A., and Turan, N. (2012). Guilt proneness and moral character. *Current Directions in Psychological Science*, 21 (5), 355–9.

Cornish, D.B. (1994).The procedural analysis of offending, and its relevance for situational prevention. In R.V. Clarke (ed.) *Crime Prevention Studies*, Volume 3. Monsey, NY: Criminal Justice Press.

Cornish, D.B., and Clarke, R.V. (1986) (Eds), *The Reasoning Criminal.* New York: Springer-Verlag.

Cornish, D.B., and Clarke, R.V. (2008). The rational choice perspective. In Wortley, R. and Mazerolle, L. (Eds) *Environmental Criminology and Crime Analysis.* Uffculme, Devon: Willan.

Coyne, J.A. (2009) *Why Evolution is True.* Oxford: Oxford University Press.

Daly, M., and Wilson, M. (1982). Whom are newborn babies said to resemble? *Ethology and Sociobiology*, 3, 69–78.

Daly, M., and Wilson, M. (1988). *Homicide.* New York: De Gruyter.

Daly, M., and Wilson, M. (1998). *The truth about Cinderella.* London: Weidenfeld and Nicolson.

Daly, M., and Wilson, M. (2005) Carpe diem: Adaptation and devaluing the future. *The Quarterly Review of Biology*, 80(1), 55–60.

Daly, M., and Wilson, M. (2007). Is the 'Cinderella effect' controversial? A case study of evolution-minded research and critiques thereof. In (eds.) C. Crawford and D. Krebs. *Foundations of evolutionary psychology*, Mahwah, NJ: Lawrence Erlbaum.

Daly, M., Wilson, M., and Weghorst, S.J. (1982). Male sexual jealousy. *Ethology and Sociobiology,* 3, 11–27.

Darwin, C. (1859). *On the origin of species by means of natural selection.* London: John Murray.

Darwin, C. (1871). *The descent of man, and selection in relation to sex.* London: John Murray.

Dawkins, R. (1976). *The selfish gene.* Oxford: Oxford University Press.

Dawkins, R. (2009). *The Greatest Show on Earth: The Evidence for Evolution.* London: Bantam.

De Waal, F. (1989) Food sharing and reciprocal obligations among chimpanzees. *Journal of Human Evolution*, 18(5), 433–459.

De Waal, F. (2009). *The age of empathy: nature's lessons for a kinder society.* New York: Harmony Books.

Decety, J. (2011). The neuroevolution of empathy. *Annals of the New York Academy of Sciences*, 1231, 35–45.

Delgado, J. (1971). The neurological basis of violence. *International Social Science Journal*, 23 (1): 27–35.

Descartes, R. (1960). *Discourse on method.* New York: Liberal Arts Press.

Dobzhansky, T. (1964). Biology, molecular and organismic. *American Zoologist*, 4 (4), 443–52.

Dollard, J. M., Doob, L.W., Miller, N.E., Mowrer O. H., and Sears, R. R. (1939). *Frustration and Aggression.* (pp. 91–109). New Haven, CT: Yale University Press.

Dunbar, K. (1995). How scientists really reason: scientific reasoning in real-world laboratories. In (eds.) R. J. Sterberg and J. E. Davidson, *The nature of insight*, pp. 365–95. Cambridge, MA: MIT Press.

Dunbar, R. I. M. (1992). Neocortex size as a constraint on group size in primates. *Journal of Human Evolution*, 22 (6), 469–93.

Duntley, J.D., and Shackleford, T.K. (2008) (eds.) *Evolutionary Forensic Psychology: Darwinian Foundations of Crime and Law*. Oxford: Oxford University Press.

Duntley, J. D., and Shackleford, T. K. (2008). Darwinian foundations of crime and law. *Aggression and Violent Behavior*, 13 (5), 373–82.

Edelman, G. (1992). *Bright Air, Brilliant Fire*. New York: Basic Books.

Ekblom, P. (2007) Making offenders richer, In Farrell, G., Bowers, K., Johnson, S. and Townsley, M. (Eds). *Imagination for Crime Prevention: Essays in Honour of Ken Pease. Crime Prevention Studies*, Vol.21. Monsey, NY: Criminal Justice Press.

Ellis, L. (2008). Reducing crime evolutionarily. In (eds.) J. D. Duntley and T. K. Shackleford. *Evolutionary forensic psychology*. Oxford: Oxford University Press.

Ellis, L., and Walsh, A. (1999). Criminologists' opinions about causes and theories of crime and delinquency. *The Criminologist*, 24 (4), 1–6.

Emery, N. J., and Clayton, N. S. (2004). The mentality of crows: convergent evolution of intelligence in corvids and apes. *Science*, 306 (5703), 1903–7.

Falk, J.H., and Balling, J.D. (2010). Evolutionary influence on human landscape preference. *Environment and Behaviour*, 42, (4), 479–493.

Farrington, D. (1986). Age and crime. In (eds.) M. Tonry and N. Morris. *Crime and justice 7*, Chicago: University of Chicago Press.

Farrington, D. (1998). Individual differences and offending. In *The handbook of crime and punishment*, (ed.) M. Tonry, pp. 241–68. New York: Oxford University Press.

Farrington, D.P. (2000). Explaining and Preventing Crime: The Globalization of Knowledge – The American Society of Criminology 1999 Presidential Address. *Criminology*, 38 (1), 1–24.

Farrington, D.P. (2002). In Maguire, M., Morgan, R., and Reiner, R. (eds.) *Oxford handbook of criminology*. Oxford: Oxford University Press.

Felson, M. (1994). *Crime and Everyday Life*. Thousand Oaks, CA: Pine Forge Press.

Felson, M., and Clarke, R.V. (1998). Opportunity Makes the Thief, *Police Research Series 98*. London: Home Office.

Feshbach, N. D. (1987). Parental empathy and child adjustment/maladjustment. In (eds.) N. Eisenberg and J. Strayer. *Empathy and its development*. Cambridge: Cambridge University Press.

Fielding, M. and Jones, V. (2012). 'Disrupting the optimal forager': predictive risk mapping and domestic burglary reduction in Trafford, Greater Manchester. *International Journal of Police Science and Management*, 14 (1), 30–41.

Foley, D., Eaves, L., Wormley, B., Silberg, J., Maes, H., Kuhn, J., and Riley, B. (2004). Childhood adversity, monoamine oxidase A genotype, and risk for conduct disorder. *Archives of General Psychiatry*, 61 (7), 738–44.

Foster, S., and Endler, J. (eds.) (1999). *Geographic variation in behavior: perspectives on evolutionary mechanisms*. New York: Oxford University Press.

Francis, R.C. (2011). *Epigenetics: the ultimate mystery of inheritance*. New York: Norton.

Galton, F. (1869). *Hereditary genius: an inquiry into its laws and consequences*. London: Julian Friedmann.

Garwood, J. (2011). A quasi-experimental investigation of self-reported offending and perception of criminal opportunity in undergraduate students. *Security Journal*, 24, 37–51

Gery, I., Miljkovitch, R., Berthoz, S., and Soussignan, R. (2009). Empathy and recognition of facial expressions of emotion in sex offenders, non-sex offenders and normal controls. *Psychiatry Research*, 165 (3), 252–62.

Getzels, J.W., and Jackson, P.W. (1962) *Creativity and Intelligence: Explorations with gifted students*. Oxford: Wiley.

Gill, M., and Pugh, L. (1964). Basal metabolism and respiration in men living at 5,800 m (19,000 ft). *Journal of Applied Physiology*, 19 (5), 949–54.

Gluckman, P., and Hanson, M. (2006). *Mismatch: the lifestyle diseases timebomb*. Oxford: Oxford University Press.

Gordon, M. B., Iglesias, J. R., Semeshenko, V., and Nadal, J. P. (2009). Crime and punishment: the economic burden of impunity. *The European Physical Journal B – Condensed Matter and Complex Systems*, 68 (1), 133–44.

Gottfredson, D.C., and Hirschi, T. (1990). *A General Theory of Crime*. Stanford, CA: Stanford University Press.

Gottfredson, M.R., and Hirschi, T. (2003). Self-control and opportunity. In Britt, C.L. and Gottfredson, M.R. (eds), *Control Theories of Crime and Delinquency. Advances in Criminological Theory, Vol.12*. New Brunswick, NJ: Transaction Publishers.

Gould, S. J. (1980). Introduction. In (ed.) B. Kurtén. *Dance of the tiger: a novel of the ice age*. New York: Random House.

Green, A. E., Kraemer, D. J. M., Fugelsang, J. A., Gray, J. R., and Dunbar, K. N. (n.d.). Connecting Long Distance: Semantic Distance in Analogical Reasoning Modulates Frontopolar Cortex Activity. *Cerebral Cortex*, 20(1), 70–76.

Griggs, J. (2012, July 26). Suicidal termites use chemical weapons to defend colony. *New Scientist*.

Gurr, T. R. (1981). Historical trends in violent crime: a critical review of the evidence. In (eds.) M. Tonry and N. Morris. *Crime and justice 3*, Chicago: University of Chicago Press.

Guttentag, M., and Secord, P. (1983). *Too many women?: the sex ratio question*. Beverly Hills: Sage.

Hamilton, W. D. (1963). The evolution of altruistic behavior. *The American Naturalist*, 97, 354–6.

Heidensohn, F. (2002). Gender and crime. In *The Oxford handbook of criminology*, 3rd edn, ed. M. Maguire. Oxford: Oxford University Press.

Hepach, R., Vaish, A., and Tomasello, M. (2012). Young children are intrinsically motivated to see others helped. *Psychological Science*, 23, 967–72.

Hesketh, T., and Xing, Z. (2006). Abnormal sex ratios in human populations: causes and consequences. *Proceedings of the National Academy of Sciences*, 103 (36), 13271–5.

Hill, M.H., and Chow, K. (2002). Life-history theory and risky-driving. *Addiction*, 97, 401–413.

Hinde, R. (1974). *Biological bases of human behaviour*. New York: McGraw-Hill.

Hirschi, T. (1986). On the compability of rational choice and control theories of crime. In Cornish, D.B. and Clarke, R.V. (eds), *The Reasoning Criminal*. New York: Springer-Verlag.

Hirschi, T., and Gottfredson, M. (1988). Towards a general theory of crime. In Buikhuisen, W. and Mednick, S.A. (Eds), *Explaining Criminal Behaviour*. Leiden: E.J.Brill.

Hogan, R. (1969). Development of an empathy scale. *Journal of Consulting and Clinical Psychology*, 33 (3), 307–16.

Hudson, L. (1966), *Contrary Imaginations: A Psychological Study of the English Schoolboy*. London: Methuen.

Hudson, S., Marshall, W. L., Wales, D., McDonald, E., Bakker, L., and McLean, A. (1993). Emotional recognition skills of sex offenders. *Annals of Sex Research*, 6 (3), 199–211.

Huesmann, L., Lefkowitz, M., and Eron, L. (1978). Sum of MMPI scales F, 4, and 9 as a measure of aggression. *Journal of Consulting and Clinical Psychology*, 46 (5), 1071–8.

Iacoboni, M. (2009). *Mirroring people: the science of empathy and how we connect with others*. New York: Picador.

Jablonka, E., and Lamb, M. (2006). *Evolution in four dimensions: genetic, epigenetic, behavioral, and symbolic variation in the history of life*. Cambridge, MA: MIT Press.

Jacquet, J., Hauert, C., Traulsen, A., and Milinski, M. (2011). Shame and honour drive cooperation. *Biology Letters*, 7, 899–901.

Jensen, G.F., and Akers, R.L. (2003). Taking social learning theory global: Micro-macro transitions in criminological theory. In Akers, R.L. and Jensen, G.F. (Eds), *Social Learning Theory and the Explanation of Crime. Advances in Criminological Theory, vol.11*. New Brunswick, NJ: Transaction Publishers.

Jensen, J. V. (1991). *Thomas Henry Huxley: communicating for science*. Newark: University of Delaware Press.

Johnson, S., and Bowers, K. (2010). Permeability and burglary risk: are cul-de-sacs safer? *Journal of Quantitative Criminology*, 26 (1), 89–111.

Johnson, S., Bernasco, W., Bowers, K., Elffers, H., Ratcliffe, J., Rengert, G., and Townsley, M. (2007). Near repeats: a cross national assessment of residential burglary. *Journal of Quantitative Criminology*, 23 (3), 201–19.

Johnson, S., Summers, L., and Pease, K. (2009). Offender as forager? A direct test of the boost account of victimization. *Journal of Quantitative Criminology*, 25 (2), 181–200.

Johnson-Laird, P. (2005). Flying bicycles: how the Wright brothers invented the airplane. *Mind and Society*, 4 (1), 27–48.

Jolliffe, D., and Farrington, D. (2004a). Empathy and offending: a systematic review and meta-analysis. *Aggression and Violent Behaviour*, 9 (5), 441–76.

Jolliffe, D., and Farrington, D. (2004b). Empathy and offending: a systematic review and meta-analysis. *Aggression and Violent Behavior*, 9 (5), 441–76.

Jones, O. (2005). Evolutionary psychology and the law. In (ed.) D. Buss. *The handbook of evolutionary psychology*, pp. 953–74. Hoboken, NJ: Wiley.

Jones, S. (2000). *Understanding violent crime*. Buckingham: Open University Press.

Kanazawa, S. (2003). A general evolutionary psychological theory of criminality and related male-typical behavior. In A. Walsh and L. Ellis (Eds.) *Biosocial Criminology: Challenging Environmentalism's Supremacy*. Hauppauge, NY: Nova Science (37–60).

Kanazawa, S. (2007). The Evolutionary Psychological Imagination: Why You Can't Get a Date On a Saturday Night and Why Most Suicide Bombers are Muslim. *Journal of Social, Evolutionary, and Cultural Psychology*, 1(2), 7–17.

Kanazawa, S., and Still, M. (2000). Why men commit crimes (and why they desist). *Sociological Theory*, 18 (3), 434–47.

Kaplan, S., and Kaplan, R. (1982). *Cognition and Environment: Functioning in an Uncertain World*. New York, Praeger.

Karniol, R. (1980). A conceptual analysis of immanent justice responses in children. *Child Development*, 51 (1), 118–30.

Kelling, G. L. and Coles, C. M. (1997) *Fixing Broken Windows*. New York: Touchstone.

Kenrick, D., and Sheets, V. (1993). Homicidal fantasies. *Ethology and Sociobiology*, 14 (4), 231–46.

Kim-Cohen, J., Caspi, A., Taylor, A., Williams, B., Newcombe, R., Craig, I., and Moffitt, T. (2006). MAOA, maltreatment, and gene–environment interaction predicting children's mental health: new evidence and a meta-analysis. *Molecular Psychiatry*, 11 (10), 903–13.

Kipling, R. (1902). *Just so stories for little children*. London: Macmillan.

Koestler, A. (1964). *The Act of Creation*. Harmondsworth: Penguin.

Krebs, J. R. (2009). The gourmet ape: evolution and human food preferences. *American Journal of Clinical Nutrition*, 90 (3), 707S–711S.

Kuhn, T. (1962). *The structure of scientific revolutions*. Chicago: University of Chicago Press.

Kushner, H. (1981). *When bad things happen to good people*. New York: Avon.

Laland, K. N., and Brown, G. R. (2002). *Sense and nonsense: evolutionary perspectives on human behaviour*. Oxford: Oxford University Press.

LeDoux, J. (1998). *The emotional brain: the mysterious underpinnings of emotional life*. New York: Simon and Schuster.

Leinisch, M. (2007). *In the beginning: fundamentalism, the Scopes trial, and the making of the antievolution movement*. Chapel Hill: University of North Carolina Press.

Lerner, M. (1980). *The belief in a just world: a fundamental delusion*. New York: Plenum.

Levesque, R. (2006). *The psychology and law of criminal justice processes*. New York: Nova.

Lorenz, K. (1966). *On aggression*. London: Methuen.

MacArthur, R. and Wilson, E. O. (1967). *The theory of island biogeography*. Princeton, NJ: Princeton University Press.

McLaughlin, E., and Muncie, J. (2001) (eds) *The Sage Dictionary of Criminology*. London, Sage.

Marshall, L. E., and Marshall, W. L. (2011). Empathy and antisocial behaviour. *Journal of Forensic Psychiatry and Psychology*, 22 (5), 742–59.

Marshall, W. L., Hudson, S., Jones, R., and Fernandez, Y. (1995). Empathy in sex offenders. *Clinical Psychology Review*, 15 (2), 99–113.

Merton, Robert K. (1938). Social structure and anomie. *American Sociological Review*, 3 (5), 672–82.

Mesquida C. G., and Wiener N. I. (1996). Human collective aggression: A behavioral ecology perspective. *Ethology and Sociobiology*, 17 (4), 247–262.

Mesquida C. G., and Wiener N. I. (1999). Male Age Composition and Severity of Conflicts. *Politics and the Life Sciences,* 18 (2), 181–189(9).

Milgram, S. (1974). *Obedience to authority: an experimental view*. New York: Harper & Row.

Miller, J. D., Scott, E. C., and Okamoto, S. (2006). Public acceptance of evolution. *Science*, 313 (5788), 765–6.

Miller, M. (2000). Homosexuality, Birth Order, and Evolution: Toward an Equilibrium Reproductive Economics of Homosexuality. *Archives of Sexual Behavior,* 29 (1), 1–34.

Miller, P. A., and Eisenberg, N. (1988). The relation of empathy to aggressive and externalizing/antisocial behavior. *Psychological Bulletin*, 103 (3), 324–44.

Mishra, S., and Lalumière, M.L. (2008). Risk-taking, anti-social behaviour and life histories. In J.D. Duntley and T.K. Shackleford (2008) (Eds.) *Evolutionary Forensic Psychology*. Oxford University Press: Oxford.

Moffett, M. (2011). Ants and the art of war. *Scientific American*, 305 (6), 84–9.

Moffitt, T. E. (1993). Adolescence-limited and life-course-persistent antisocial behavior: a developmental taxonomy, *Psychological Review*, 100 (4), 674–701.

Moffitt, T. E. (1994). Natural histories of delinquency. In *Cross-national longitudinal research on human development and criminal behavior*, (eds.) E. Weitekamp and H. Kerner. Dordrecht: Kluwer Academic Press.

Moffitt, T.E. (2003). Life-course persistent and adolescence-limited antisocial behaviour: A research review and a research agenda. In B. Lahey, T.E.Moffitt and A. Caspi (eds) *The Causes of Conduct Disorder and Serious Juvenile Delinquency*. New York: Guildford.

Moll, J., Krueger, F., Zahn, R., Pardini, M., de Oliveira-Souza, R., and Grafman, J. (2006). Human fronto-mesolimbic networks guide decisions about charitable donation. *Proceedings of the National Academy of Sciences*, 103 (42), 15623–8.

Morrison, H., and Goldberg, H. (2004). *My life among the serial killers: inside the minds of the world's most notorious murderers*. Chichester: Wiley.

Morrissey, M., and Pease, K. (1982). The black criminal justice system in west Belfast. *Howard Journal of Criminal Justice*, 21 (1–3), 159–66.

Murdock, G. (1945). The common denominator of cultures. In (ed.) R. Linton. *The science of man in the world crisis*, New York: Columbia University Press.

Nagin, D. and Tremblay, R. (1999). Trajectories of boys' physical aggression, opposition, and hyperactivity on the path to physically violent and nonviolent juvenile delinquency. *Child Development*, 70 (5), 1181–96.

Naismith, D. J. (1969). The foetus as a parasite. *Proceedings of the Nutrition Society*, 28 (1), 25–31.

Newburn, T. (2007). *Criminology*. Cullompton, Devon: Willan.

Newman, O. (1972) *Defensible Space*. NewYork: Macmillan.

Norman, D. (1998). *The Design of Everyday Things*. London: MIT Press.

Nowak, M., with Highfield, R. (2011). *Super cooperators: evolution, altruism and human behaviour or why we need each other to succeed*. Edinburgh: Canongate.

Oates, K., and Wilson, M. (2002). Nominal kinship cues facilitate altruism. *Proceedings of the Royal Society London B*, 269 (1487), 105–9.

Okasha, S. (2006). *Evolution and the levels of selection*. Oxford: Clarendon.

Oldroyd, D. R. (1983). *Darwinian impacts: an introduction to the Darwinian revolution,* 2nd edn. Milton Keynes: Open University Press.

Orians, G.H., and Heerwagen, J.H. (1992). Evolved responses to landscapes. In Barkow, J.H., Cosmides, L. and Tooby, J. (Eds) *The Adapted Mind: Evolutionary Psychology and the Generation of Culture*. Oxford, Oxford University Press.

Ormerod, D. (2011). *Smith and Hogan's criminal law*, 13th edn. Oxford: Oxford University Press.

Pagel, M. (2012). *Wired for culture*. London: Allen Lane.

Palmer, C.T., and Tilley, C.F. (1995). Sexual access to females as a motivation for joining gangs: An evolutionary approach. *The Journal of Sex Research*, (32), 213–217.

Pease, K. (1988). *Judgements of crime seriousness: findings from the 1984 British crime survey*. London: Home Office.

Pease, K. (2006). No through road: closing pathways to crime. In K. Moss, and M. Stephens (Eds.) *Crime Reduction and the Law*. Abingdon, Oxon: Routledge.

Pease, K., Ireson, J., and Thorpe, J. (1975). Modified crime indices for eight countries. *The Journal of Criminal Law and Criminology*, 66 (2), 209–14.

Petersen, M., Sell, A., Tooby, J., and Cosmides, L. (2010). Evolutionary psychology and criminal justice: a recalibrational theory of punishment and reconciliation. In (ed.) H. Høgh-Olesen. *Human morality and sociality*, pp. 73–131. New York: Palgrave Macmillan.

Phillips, D.P., Ruth, T.E., and Wagner, L.M. (1993). Psychology and survival. *The Lancet*, 342,1142–1145.

Piaget, J. (1932). *The moral judgment of the child.* London: Kegan Paul.

Pillard, R. C., and Bailey, J. M. (1998). Human sexual attraction has a heritable component. *Human Biology,* 70 (2), 347–65.

Pillow, B. H. (1991). Children's understanding of biased social cognition. *Developmental Psychology,* 27 (4), 539–51.

Pinker, S. (2002). *The blank slate: the modern denial of human nature.* London: Allen Lane.

Pinker, S. (2011). *The better angels of our nature: the decline of violence in history and its causes.* London: Allen Lane.

Piquero, A. and Moffitt, T. (2004). Life-course persistent offending. In (ed.) J. Adler. *Forensic psychology: concepts, debates and practice,* pp. 177–96. Cullompton, Devon: Willan.

Premack, D., and Woodruff, G. (1978). Does the chimpanzee have a theory of mind? *Behavioral and Brain Sciences,* 1 (4), 515–26.

Profet, M. (1992). Pregnancy Sickness as Adaptation: A deterrent to Maternal Ingestion of Teratogens. In Barkow J.H. *et al* (eds) *The Adapted Mind Adapted.* Oxford: Oxford University Press.

Quinlan, R. J. (2007). Human parental effort and environmental risk. *Proceedings of the Royal Society London B,* 274 (1606), 121–5.

Raman, L., and Winer, G. (2002). Children's and adults' understanding of illness: evidence in support of a coexistence model. *Genetic, Social, and General Psychology Monographs,* 128 (4), 325–55.

Raman, L., and Winer, G. (2004). Evidence of more immanent justice responding in adults than children: a challenge to traditional developmental theories. *British Journal of Developmental Psychology,* 22 (2), 255–74.

Reiss, A.J. (1986). Why are communities important in understanding crime? In Reiss, A.J. and Tonry, M. (eds), *Communities and Crime. Crime and Justice: A Review of Research,* Vol. 8. Chicago: University of Chicago Press.

Roach, J. (2012). Terrorists, Affordance and the Over-Estimation of Offence Homogeneity. In M. Taylor and P.M. Currie (eds.) *Terrorism and Affordance.* London: Continuum.

Roach, J., Ekblom, P., and Flynn, R. (2005). The conjunction of terrorist opportunity: a framework for diagnosing and preventing acts of terrorism. *Security Journal,* 18 (3), 7–25.

Roach, J. and Pease, K. (2011). Evolution and the prevention of violent crime. *Psychology,* 2 (4), 393–404.

Ross, N., and Pease, K. (2008). Community policing and prediction. In (ed.) T. Williamson. *The handbook of knowledge-based policing.* Chichester: Wiley.

Ross, R., and Ross, R. (1995). *Thinking straight: the reasoning and rehabilitation program for delinquency prevention and offender rehabilitation.* Ottawa: Air Training and Publications.

Schneier, B. (2012). *Liars and outliers: enabling the trust that society needs to thrive.* Indianapolis, IN: Wiley.

Sear, R., Mace, R., and McGregor, I. A. (2000). Maternal grandmothers improve nutritional status and survival of children in rural Gambia. *Proceedings of the Royal Society B,* 267 (1453), 1641–7.

Sidebottom, A., and Tilley, N. (2008). Evolutionary psychology and fear of crime. *Policing* (2008) 2 (2), 167–174.

Singer, T., Seymour, B., O'Doherty, J., Stephan, K., Dolan, R., and Frith, C. (2006). Empathic neural responses are modulated by the perceived fairness of others. *Nature,* 439 (7075), 466–9.

Slote, M. (2011). The philosophy of empathy. *Phi Kappa Phi Forum*, 91 (1), 13–15.

Smith, B., and Stevens, R. (2002) Evolutionary psychology. In Miell, D., Phoenix, A. and Thomas, K. (Eds) *Mapping Psychology 1*, Milton Keynes: Open University Press.

Smuts, B. (1992). Male aggression against women: an evolutionary perspective. *Human Nature,* 3 (1), 1–44.

Sober, E., and Wilson, D. S. (1998). *Unto others: the evolution and psychology of unselfish behaviour*. Cambridge, MA: Harvard University Press.

Spector, T. (2012). *Identically different: why you can change your genes*. London: Weidenfeld and Nicolson.

Spencer, H. (1870). *Principles of psychology*, 2nd edn. London: Willams and Norgate.

Stoks, F.G. (1983). Assessing urban space environments for danger of violent crime–especially rape (cited in Orians and Heerwagen, 1992 op. cit.).

Stylianou, S. (2003). Measuring crime seriousness perceptions: what have we learned and what else do we want to know? *Journal of Criminal Justice*, 31 (1), 37–56.

Summers, L., Johnson, S., and Pease, K. (2007). The contagion of theft of and theft from motor vehicles: applications of epidemiological techniques. *Revista Electrónica de Investigación Criminológica*, 5 (1), 1–22.

Sykes,G.M., and Matza, D. (1957) Techniques of neutralization: a theory of delinquency. *American Sociological Review*, (22), 664–70.

Tajfel, H. (1981). *Human groups and social categories: studies in social psychology*. Cambridge: Cambridge University Press.

Taylor, C., and Meenaghan, A. (2006) Expert Decision making in Burglars. *British Journal of Criminology*, Vol. 46, 935–949.

Thompson, E. (1972). Rough music: the English charivari. *Annales*, 27, 285–312.

Thornhill, R., and Thornhill, N.W. (1983) Human rape: An evolutionary analysis. *Ethology and Sociobiology*, (4), 137–173.

Townsley, M., Johnson, S., and Ratcliffe, J. (2008). Space time dynamics of insurgent activity in Iraq. *Security Journal*, 21 (3), 139–46.

Trivers, R. L. (1971). The evolution of reciprocal altruism. *Quarterly Review of Biology*, 46 (1), 35–57.

Trivers, R. L. (2011). *Deceit and self-deception: fooling yourself the better to fool others*. London: Allen Lane.

Walsh, A., and Beaver, K.M. (2009) (Eds.). *Biosocial Criminology: New Directions in Theory and Research*. New York: Routledge.

Walsh,A., and Ellis, L. (2003)(Eds.). *Biosocial criminology: challenging environmentalism's supremacy*. New York: Nova.

Walsh, A., and Ellis, L. (2007). *Criminology: an interdisciplinary approach*. Thousand Oaks, CA: Sage.

Whitam, F. L. (1983). Culturally invariable properties of male homosexuality: tentative conclusions from cross-cultural research. *Archives of Sexual Behavior*, 12 (3), 207–26.

Whyte, W.H. (1980) *The social life of small urban spaces*. Washington, DC: Conservation Foundation.

Wiksröm, P-O. H. (2005). The social origins of pathways in crime: Towards a developmental ecological action theory of crime involvement and its changes. In Farrington, D.P. (Ed.) Integrated Developmental & Life-Course Theories of Offending, *Advances in Criminological Theory*, Volume 14. New Brunswick, NJ: Transaction Publishers.

Wilkinson, G. (1984). Reciprocal food sharing in the vampire bat. *Nature*, 308, 181–4.

Wilkinson, G. (1988). Reciprocal altruism in bats and other mammals. *Ethology and Sociobiology*, 9 (2), 85–100.

Wilson, D. S. (1975). A theory of group selection. *Proceedings of the National Academy of Sciences*, 72 (1), 143–6.

Wilson, E. O. (1978). *On human nature*. Cambridge, MA: Harvard University Press.

Wilson, E. O. (1994). *Naturalist*. Washington, DC: Island Press.

Wilson, E. O. (2012). *The social conquest of earth*. New York: Liveright.

Wilson, M., and Daly, M. (1985). Competitiveness, risk-taking, and violence: The young male syndrome. *Ethology and Sociobiology*, 6, 59–73.

Wilson, M., and Daly, M. (1996). Male sexual proprietariness and violence against women. *Current Directions in Psychological Science*, 5, 2–7.

Wilson, M., and Daly, M. (2006). Are juvenile offenders extreme future discounters? *Psychological Science*, 17(11), 989–994.

Wilson, M., Daly, M., and Pound, N. (2002). An evolutionary psychological perspective on the modulation of competitive confrontation and risk-taking. *Hormones, Brain and Behavior*, 5, 381–408.

Wimmer, H., and Perner, J. (1983). Beliefs about beliefs: representation and constraining function of wrong beliefs in young children's understanding of deception. *Cognition*, 13 (1), 103–28.

Wortley, R. (2001). A classification of techniques for controlling situational precipitators of crime. *Security Journal*, (14) 63–82.

Wortley, R. (2011). *Psychological criminology: an integrative approach*. London: Routledge.

Wortley, R., and Mazerolle, L. (2008) (Eds.) *Environmental Criminology and Crime Analysis*. Cullompton, Devon: Willan.

Woyciechowski, M., and Kozlowski, J. (1998). Division of labor by division of risk according to worker life expectancy in the honeybee (Apis mellifera L.). *Apidologie,* 29 (1–2), 191–205.

Wright R. (1994) *The Moral Animal*. London: Abacus.

Youstin, T., Nobles, M., Ward, J., and Cook, C. (2011). Assessing the generalizability of the near repeat phenomenon. *Criminal Justice and Behavior*, 38 (10), 1042–63.

Zahn-Waxler, C., and Robinson, J. (1995). Empathy and guilt: early origins of feelings of responsibility. In *Self-conscious emotions: the psychology of shame, guilt, embarrassment and pride*, (ed.) J. P. Tangney and K. W. Fisher. New York: Guilford.

Zimbardo, P. (2007). *The Lucifer effect: understanding how good people turn evil*. New York: Random House.

Zimbardo, P. G. (1973). *A Field Experiment in Auto-shaping*. In Ward, C. (Ed) Vandalism. London: Architectural Press.

Zinn, W. (1993). The empathic physician. *Archives of Internal Medicine*, 153 (3), 306–12.

Index